HOW TO
WIN FRIENDS
AND
INFLUENCE
ENEMIES

*Taking On Liberal Arguments
with Logic and Humor*

Will Witt

CENTER
STREET

NEW YORK   NASHVIL

Center Street
Hachette Book Group
1290 Avenue of the Americas, New York, NY 10104
centerstreet.com
twitter.com/centerstreet

First Edition: September 2021

Center Street is a division of Hachette Book Group, Inc. The Center Street name and logo are trademarks of Hachette Book Group, Inc.

The publisher is not responsible for websites (or their content) that are not owned by the publisher.

The Hachette Speakers Bureau provides a wide range of authors for speaking events. To find out more, go to www.HachetteSpeakersBureau.com or call (866) 376-6591.

Library of Congress Control Number: 2021939218

ISBNs: 9781546000242 (hardcover), 9781546000273 (ebook)

Printed in the United States of America

LSC-C

Printing 1, 2021

HOW TO
WIN FRIENDS
AND
INFLUENCE
ENEMIES

To my grandpa Chocolate, who taught me what it means to be a man and helped me become a leader.

Contents

· · · · · · · · · ·

CONTENTS

HOW TO
WIN FRIENDS
AND
INFLUENCE
ENEMIES

Introduction

WHY
CONSERVATIVES
LOSE

G OD IS DEAD. God remains dead. And we have killed him."

Many people read this Friederich Nietzsche quote as a celebration of the collapse of the monotheistic worldview in the west. Young atheists champion this phrase as a heroic pronouncement, that the destruction of God and these types of worldviews are something to be cheered and applauded. But in reality, this is a misinterpretation. Nietzche said this in grieving, referring to the removal of Christian morality from the west and its replacement with scientific discovery and government control. Nietzsche knew that without the belief system imposed on us from Christianity, the world would face certain collapse.

Although Nietzsche was in fact an atheist most of his life, he understood the importance of a belief system to bring cohesiveness to a group of people. Nietzsche realized that although "God was dead," people would find a replacement for that system of beliefs.

Enter leftism. Although Europe and America became more and more secular throughout the 20th century, there was no shortage of belief systems and "religions" that people latched on to to give their lives some sort of meaning. Whether it was communism, the environmental movement, Malthusianism, or any other system of belief, people found solace in their "herd morality," and their impacts have had long-lasting and detrimental effects on the world as a whole.

Leftism has become the dominant religion in America. It is quite ironic that Karl Marx claimed, "Religion is the opium of the people," while leftism and many of the principles he preached have become the ascendent dogmatic beliefs throughout western culture. And just like any other religion, it has a set of values. The tenets of this faith are that you stand against inequality, you stand against hate, you love the earth. These are some of the commandments the church of leftism preaches, and they sound pretty good, right? I mean, who isn't against hate? Who doesn't love the earth? These values sound like a wonderful way to live life, that is, until you put them into practice through the lens of leftism. Fighting against inequality becomes demonizing the successful. Standing against hate means silencing and attacking anyone who disagrees with you. Loving the earth translates to humans being parasites on our planet.

Also akin to other belief systems, there are consequences for "sinning" within this religion. If you go against the dominant agenda, you will be "canceled" and slandered by the mob. If you don't post a black square on Instagram in support of Black Lives Matter, you are a racist bigot who should be shamed. If you choose to throw away your plastic straw instead of recycling it, you are an immoral person who is killing the planet.

What's even more ironic is that I used to be a disciple of the church of leftism. I grew up in a household where my father was never there; he was in prison for most of my childhood, and so I was raised primarily by my mom and older brother, who was my half brother. My older brother Zach acted the role of father for me, and I took everything he said as fact, so when he made claims, such as "politics is all a waste of time" or "God and religion are stupid," I took these things incredibly to heart. I became a politically apathetic atheist for most of my life, eating up the leftist religion my teachers and peers preached and making it my primary belief system. When I got to high school, I ended up interning for a Democratic state senator, who pushed me over the edge even further. At that point in my life, I couldn't tell you what the difference between a Republican and a Democrat was, I couldn't tell you what socialism was, and I couldn't tell you what the First Amendment was. But I could tell you that global warming was a catastrophe, I could tell you that cops were racist, and I could tell you how stupid God and Christianity were.

It is important to note at this point in my life story that I wasn't a happy person. Throughout high school I felt like my life had no purpose. I partied all the time, most of my friends were terrible influences, and my relationships with my family members were shaky at best. I tried to find meaning in my life in all sorts of different places, various girls, odd jobs, and partying, and none of them did anything to make my life seem worthwhile. I was depressed on the inside, but on the outside, I was the poster child for your next president of Young Democrats of America.

But everything changed when I finally graduated high school and made it to university. For the first part of college, I was as depressed as ever and continuing my antics, exponentially increasing the levels at which I performed them and growing more and more hollow with each passing day. My connection with my mom was worse than ever, and I disregarded my family as a hindrance to my success. I ended up failing many of my classes, blaming the world for being unfair, and victimizing myself for my circumstances. Things seemed to be at a dead end for me, that is, until I entered the classroom for one of my most left-wing classes.

The class was Sociology 101, a class that conservatives today reference to justify the assertion that universities are brainwashing the youth of America, and justly so. This class ticked every leftist propaganda checklist. White privilege? Check. Sexism and the patriarchy? Check. Capitalism sucks? Double check. This class was complete leftist garbage, but at the time, I had no idea I was being brainwashed. That was until one day in class, when I sat next to this nice black girl in my class. The topic of the day was how African Americans had been oppressed for centuries by the white man and how they are still being oppressed. I listened to my teacher, nodding along and understanding the things she said, until she pointed at me. She stuck a finger out at me and then pointed a finger at the black girl sitting next to me and said something I will never forget: "You are oppressing this girl next to you because of the color of your skin."

I was shocked. I looked at the black girl sitting next to me, and she shrugged at me, feeling just as awkward as I did in that situation. I didn't say anything; I just sat there in my lecture hall chair until the class was over.

I remember being on the bus on my way back thinking about what she had said to me. *Was I really oppressing these black people? I never felt like I was oppressing black people. The black girl seemed just as weirded out as I was. She couldn't possibly think I was oppressing her, could she?* All these questions raced through my mind at a million miles an hour, and I was mortified by the fact that I could be oppressing all these people. I didn't know it at the time, but this was the first groundbreaking moment on my path to realizing my brainwashing.

After that class and experience were over, I didn't think a whole lot about the issue until 2016, when Donald Trump was running for president. I started to see how controversial it was to support Donald Trump, but I didn't realize why yet. It wasn't until the girl I was seeing at the time and I got into a political argument that I realized what was happening in America. We got into an argument about something mundane, I think immigration, and I remember saying that illegal immigration was a bad thing. I then remember her saying something that changed my life forever: "You sound like a Trump supporter." I had never thought of myself in that way, but in that moment, I did. I turned back to her and said, "You know what, maybe I am." After this argument, and our subsequent breakup after this "chat," I started getting incredibly political. I started working with the Republican Party in Colorado, I started working with Turning Point USA and other student groups, and eventually I found out about PragerU and its online videos. I binge-watched every one of its videos, and I started skipping class to go outside on my campus and table and debate students about politics. Yeah, I was that guy. Even my professors would walk by from the classes I missed and shake their heads seeing me out in the quad talking to people and skipping their lectures. But I just shrugged my shoulders and continued doing what I was doing. I knew what I was doing was more important than some intro to philosophy class or some English class talking about how terrible white men were. I had a vision of what I wanted to do, and I made that vision a reality.

I ended up making a video on my campus in which I asked girls what they thought about the wage gap, and of course they all thought they were incredibly oppressed. I borrowed my buddy's GoPro to shoot the video, taught myself how to edit, and sent the finished product to PragerU. Looking back now, it wasn't a great video, and my skills at talking to people and editing were subpar at best, but still PragerU saw something in me and offered me a job when I was done with my sophomore year of college.

I ended up staying in Colorado for a while to do some

work there for a bit and then decided to drop out of college and move out to Los Angeles to live out my dream with PragerU. My mom was upset at me for my decision, my grandparents were scared for my future, and everyone I knew at the time thought I would fail and never make it, but I knew I had a bigger purpose. I remember kids from high school and college talking behind my back all over social media, saying I was "a racist conservative now" and that I would never make anything of myself without getting my degree. I'm happy to report now that everything I said I was going to do I have done, and I have been much better off leaving college than staying in it and finishing it with a degree that wouldn't do me any good.

My videos now have over 500 million views, I have a successful podcast with thousands of listeners, I have produced multiple mini-documentaries, I have worked with some of the biggest political voices in the world, and I have educated and changed the minds of thousands of people. I don't say all of this to gloat or brag to all of you; I say it to show you what is wrong with conservatives nowadays and why we lose so often. Conservatives are weak and don't stand up for what they believe in. They give in to the left and go along with the current culture we see in America instead of standing up to the horrible things we see destroying and corrupting our nation. They are afraid—sometimes for good reason, don't get me wrong—to stand up and get canceled or fired or ostracized or to lose friends or family for saying what they believe. We also see Republicans in Congress who claim to fight for our values or say they're going to defend our beliefs when in reality they are bought out by corporations or special interests and do the exact opposite of what they promised on the campaign trail. The point is, there is this stigma with conservatives nowadays that says, "It's so hard to be a conservative" or "I can't stand up for what I believe in because it's too hard" or "I'll be better off if I just keep quiet." I bring up all that I have accomplished to show that there is no strength in silence. I stood up for what I believed in, and now my life is amazing and I am influencing millions of people and changing thousands upon thousands of minds.

What I have come to realize is that the same people who are worried about what the left will do to them if they speak up now should be far more worried about what the left will do to them if they *don't* speak up now. We are in a civil war for ideas in this country, and the only way to fight back is to actually fight back. I decided to speak up, and I dropped out of school and moved to a new city with no money and knowing no one to be that fighter. I'm of course not saying you have to take the same path as I did, but what I am saying is that in all of these situations of doubt and trial, you have to stand up for what you know is right, or I guarantee everything you hold dear will be lost. With this book, I am going to arm you with the knowledge and tactics and skills to do your best to fight back against the leftist dogma we hear from so many people, and you will be able to change the minds of all the people around you pushing their liberal ideas.

It is easy to stay silent and say nothing, but I promise you that if you choose to do that, America will be lost. There is no better time to stand up and be a fighter than right now, and I fear that if we don't, our very way of life, the traditional American values we know and need, will be gone forever. Ten years from now, do you want to look back on your life and say I was someone who stood back and watched my country crumble around me, or do you want to look back at how hard you fought and know that you secured a better America for generations to come? I know what I would choose, and I ask all of you now to do the same. Do you choose to be the fighter and stand up for your values, or are you going to sit back silently? I pray you make the right choice because I'm not going to lie to you—we need all the help we can get.

Chapter 1

....

RACISM

NOT A DAY goes by when I am not called a racist. Every day on social media perusing my comments and mentions, there is without fail some leftist who calls me a racist for my conservative views. If I make a video about the truth about police brutality, I'm a racist. If I write a tweet about standing up for my values, I'm a racist. If I post an Instagram story about how much I love Chipotle, I'm a racist.

Today, racism is *the* issue that leftists cling to more than any other. They use the moniker "racist" to shame anyone who has a different point of view—or, in my case, enjoys tacos from a popular Mexican fast-food restaurant. The largest institutions in America—by which I mean universities, the mainstream media, and Hollywood—continue to spread the lie that America is a horrible, racist place. Young people across the country are lashing out in defiance of this so-called racism.

America is on fire. Leftists across the country are violently protesting and rioting throughout various American cities, destroying businesses and people's livelihoods, and they're doing it all in the name of "racial justice." They loot and steal from stores and wreck their own neighborhoods because, for some reason, they believe that doing so will bring about equality. But when you take a moment to actually look at what the left is doing in this country through a clear lens, you can easily see how counterintuitive everything they are doing is. They claim to stand up for minorities while they terrorize black business owners and decimate their stores. They claim to stand for diversity despite the fact that an overwhelming majority of Black Lives Matter protestors are actually white. In my home city of Los Angeles, for instance, over 90 percent of the people who took to the streets in support of Black Lives Matter were of Caucasian descent. But despite the hypocrisy in their claims, the left continues to scream "RACISM" as loud as they can. Even worse, they shame people around them who don't stand against this so-called racism in the same way that they do.

When I was in high school, one of the main books I had to read for my Advanced Placement U.S. History class was *A People's History of the United States* by Howard Zinn. If you've taken a history class lately, especially if that history class was part of a public high school curriculum, you've probably had to read this book, too. There's a reason for that. Today, much of the public-school curriculum is written by leftists, and there is no book, in my mind, that tickles their delicate, anti-American sensibilities more than Howard Zinn's. The book is full of anti-American sentiments, dealing with America's past and painting the United States as the worst country ever to exist. It is a book that claims to know everything about the history of the United States; it doesn't ask questions or deal in nuance the way good history is supposed to. Instead, it gives answers, and those answers are scary.

In the book, Zinn draws a direct line from Christopher Columbus, who he believes was little more than a heartless, money-hungry murderer; to the Founding Fathers, who he says are racist; to Andrew Jackson, an evil, violent racist; right up to the dropping of the atomic bomb in 1945, which, according to the book, is the most serious war crime ever committed. It does not matter to Zinn that these events also contributed to the United States' rarefied place on the world stage or that several of them—particularly the atomic bomb— were strategically necessary to spread freedom and democracy around the world. For anyone interested in an extremely thorough and precise takedown of this ridiculous book, I would recommend the article "Undue Certainty," written by an academic named Sam Wineburg in the magazine *American Educator.*

"A history of unalloyed certainties is dangerous because it invites a slide into intellectual fascism," he writes. "History as truth, issued from the left or from the right, abhors shades of gray. It seeks to stamp out the democratic insight that people of good will can see the same thing and come to different conclusions... Such a history atrophies our tolerance for complexity. It makes us allergic to exceptions to the rule. Worst of all, it depletes the moral courage we need to revise our beliefs in the face of new evidence. It ensures, ultimately, that tomorrow we will think exactly as we thought yesterday— and the day before, and the day before that."

Of course, I wasn't thinking that way when I was in high school. I was young and angry, ready to believe whatever hateful, anti-American rhetoric the school system had to throw at me. I remember reading Zinn's book and thinking that the country I lived in was terrible. I felt ashamed to be a citizen of such an evil nation.

Eventually, I came to realize the numerous errors in this book, many of which went far beyond the usual framing or interpretive errors of bad history. These appeared to me to be mistakes of fact—some of which were very basic. Zinn, for example, writes that the fire-bombing of Dresden, which occurred in 1945, happened "at the start of World War II." Huh. Maybe I learned this wrong, but I thought that 1945 was pretty close to the *end* of World War II. This may seem minor, but it does beg the question: If this guy could screw up something that basic, what else did he get wrong?

Beyond problems with a single book, I also realized some of the lies within the revisionist history my teacher was preaching. Most of my fellow classmates weren't so lucky. This book and its similar ideals, such as the 1619 project, which is the teaching that America was actually founded in 1619 when the first slaves came to Virginia, not 1776, now being mandatory teaching in some schools across the nation, are being taught across the country in almost every class where history is taught. It's no wonder that these young protestors are out marching and rioting for something they don't understand.

When talking to people on the left about racism, you will hear some very common tropes. *America is a racist country. The effects of slavery are still present today. Institutions across the country are set up to keep minorities down.* I'm sure you've heard these statements before. The left pops these blanket statements out like a PEZ dispenser, citing racism whenever you see inequality in America.

The left claims our country was founded on racism and that even our Founding Fathers intended our country to be racist.

But is that really the case? What can history tell us about how the Founding Fathers established this nation?

Let's first address the elephant in the room. Yes, many of the Founding Fathers had slaves. Thomas Jefferson, George Washington, and other Founding Fathers owned slaves; this is something most people would know. But did you know that many of the Founding Fathers had just inherited their slaves? Did you know Thomas Jefferson had relations with a black woman and had children with her, who he made free? Or that he went against the crown and taught his slaves to read and write? Or did you know John Adams refused to own slaves? There are many things about the Founding Fathers and their relationships with slaves that are glossed over in American history class because they don't fit the mainstream leftist agenda. George Washington said, "I can only say that there is not a man living who wishes more sincerely than I do to see a plan adopted for the abolition of [slavery]," and many other founders agreed with his sentiment. Benjamin Franklin even helped start the first ever anti-slavery society in 1774 in New York. Yet despite all the evidence pointing to the fact that many of the founders were heavily opposed to slavery, the narrative still exists today that America was founded by racists who loved slavery and hated black people, which frankly just isn't true.

Was America founded to give equality to everyone? Or was it founded as a racist nation only benefiting white people? Well, let's look at the Declaration of Independence. Actually, let's go even further back and look at Thomas Jefferson's draft of the Declaration of Independence. The Declaration of Independence that we all know today reads as follows: "We hold these truths to be self-evident, that all men are created equal, that they are endowed by their Creator with certain unalienable Rights, that among these are Life, Liberty and the pursuit of Happiness." In Thomas Jefferson's draft of the Declaration, though, there is one major difference: "the pursuit of Happiness" is replaced with "Property." So why did they change this at the last minute to what made the final cut? They changed it because they knew that many southern states would look at the Declaration of Independence fully believing that their slaves were property, thinking that God gave them the right to have them. The Founding Fathers changed this wording in the final Declaration because they did not believe that slaves were endowed to every man by their creator; they believed they were men all on their own. Seems pretty progressive and transformative for the time for a bunch of white, slave-owning racists, right?

Despite all of this, it is still fair to say that there was racism during the founding of this country. Slavery was abhorrent, and many people still believed black people were less, but another lie that persists is that slavery is what built this country and the institution of it still echoes throughout society today.

In America today, you have just as equal an opportunity to make a wonderful life for yourself as anyone else, regardless of your race. Racism is not the issue in America the left would like to paint it as and has been largely solved throughout this country. What is the real kicker is that the left, who cry "racism" every chance they get, don't do anything to actually help black people. Posting a black square on your Instagram doesn't help black people. Calling Aunt Jemima syrup racist doesn't help black people. If these people really wanted to affect the outcomes of black people's lives in America, they would be advocating for school choice. If they really cared one bit about the success of black people in America, they would stop virtue signaling on social media and start advocating against affirmative action and the welfare state and become champions for family values and fathers in the home.

RACISM

The biggest factor in America that determines economic mobility is marriage; our current welfare state in America disincentivizes marriage heavily, and black people in America are the most likely group to be on welfare. Despite African Americans making up 13.4 percent of the U.S. population, they account for 39.8 percent of all welfare recipients in America, according to the U.S. Department of Health and Human Services, which is heavily affected by their marriage rates and out-of-wedlock births. According to the U.S. Census, 72 percent of all black babies born are from single mothers. Single mothers are better off not getting married due to getting better benefits in our current welfare system, and so men have no responsibility to the women they knock up, creating a broken cycle that is the most prominent in black communities. Growing up without a father is seen to have a huge effect on how children grow up as well. According to data from the U.S. Department of Justice, children from fatherless homes account for 63 percent of youth suicides, 90 percent of all homeless and runaway youth, 85 percent of all children who experience behavioral disorders, and 71 percent of all high school dropouts. Although this study was completed in 1998, the same holds true today, as seen in a 2016 study that showed that 45 percent of kids in juvenile detention centers grew up in single-parent households, compared to only 30 percent for two-parent households.

Black people being worse off in America than white people is not some big ploy by the evil racists of our society; it is a larger problem with many deep-rooted issues that have all come about from big government programs and "war on poverty" efforts. Let's look at the numbers concerning actual racism in America. In 1940, 60 percent of black women were domestic servants. That rate is 2.2 percent today. In 1958, 44 percent of whites said they would move if a black person became their neighbor. Today that number is down to 1 percent. Only 18 percent of whites in 1964 said they had a black friend, and today that number is 86 percent. People are obviously less racist today than they were decades ago, but the myths about America being a racist place persist, and the even more insidious lie that racism keeps black people down in America is even more prevalent.

The left claims that the pillars of America—the universities, the economy, and the media—are all controlled by an overarching racist agenda. They claim blacks in America are kept down because of this "institutional racism." But after looking at the data, it's easy to understand that economic issues within black communities like the welfare state and fatherlessness are the real issues hindering black people's success in America, not evil, racist shadow institutions. Of course, there is still a degree of racism out there. There are still racist people out there. But to make broad assumptions about our country as a whole without pointing at specific examples of racism is a fault and is what ultimately contributes to the vast division in our country. Our country elected a black man as president, twice! How racist as a whole could we really be or how terrible could our institutions be if this happened? It can only be that the left is wrong about racism in this country, that racism is mostly solved, and that the issues facing minority communities are due to economic and cultural issues, not race-related ones.

The left is caught up on race. Rioters are destroying this country because of the issue of race. Every issue, every example of inequality can be traced back to racism by the left, but not by conservatives. Conservatives realize that for our country to be the best, every single person living in it has to be the best. Conservatives know that when minorities succeed, our country succeeds, and push to give every person in America an equal opportunity to live out their American dream. So how do we convince people who disagree on the issue of racism that America is the best place to be if you're a minority?

Well, since this is the first chapter, let's talk about strategy first.

· · · · ·

When it comes to changing minds, you have to be very careful. If you push too hard, you'll end up alienating the person you're talking to even further. If you don't push hard enough, the person you're speaking with won't learn anything. They also might run you over with their own arguments. You have to find the perfect middle ground between debating and questioning that gives you enough ammunition to give them the correct information while asking them questions that are thought-provoking and challenge the person's previously held views. In many of the debates and interviews I have done, I finish the conversation, and the people I talked to didn't even know I was a conservative despite now having their mind opened up to a totally new way of thinking. The key principle to remember when it comes to changing minds is that YOU are NOT the person to change their mind. THEY change their OWN mind by how you ask them to support their own information. If you ask them a question about racism and they don't have the answer, that is a teaching moment because they could not come up with the counter information themselves.

If you tell them a fact about racism and tell them that you are right, they are put in a defensive position where their mind is closed to being changed and can only think about how to refute you. Asking questions that lead them into expressing their own ideas is how you change minds, not by just blankly telling them the information. When they have to think about something new themselves with a question that is calm and non-threatening, they will be very open to learning something new and changing their mind.

All of this takes a lot of practice. Don't be upset if you're not a mind-changing wizard the first time you try to do this; I for sure wasn't. It took me a really long time to fine-tune my skills as a debater. It was not easy to learn to debate people who vehemently disagreed with me, had bad attitudes, or weren't understanding without getting mad myself in the process. But now after practicing and refining my debate and interview skills, I am confident in any situation where I am talking to someone with a difference of opinion or a person whose mind I'm directly trying to change. But the right way to ask questions and debate tactics isn't enough on its own to convert people; you also have to have the facts and the *right* questions. I wrote this book to give you the tools to practice with and change minds on all of the biggest issues of the day so everyone can be successful talking to people who disagree with them. When it comes to racism, there are a lot of great questions to ask to lead them into an open mind using many of the facts discussed previously.

What is important to hit on here is the left's hypocrisy when it comes to how terrible America is. They claim it is such an evil, racist place yet refuse to leave. One of the best questions to ask off the bat is, "Where in the world would you rather live than America?" or "What country is better to live in as a minority than America?" Again, as a reminder, you are asking these questions really trying to get their answer, not condescendingly to put them on the defensive. Many people when asked this question will claim they would rather live in some European country, specifically Nordic countries, and claim that they are less racist. What's funny is that when looking at racially tolerant countries, America ranks among the best, and many European countries rank as much less tolerant. According to the *Washington Post*, a country like France is among the most racially intolerant countries in the world, with 22.7 percent of people in France claiming they wouldn't want to live near someone of a different race. The Nordic countries did score very low for racial intolerance, yet these countries are some of the most racially homogenous countries on the planet, like Finland with a native Finnish population of 87.3 percent or Norway with 86.3 percent of its population being ethnic Norwegians. So, the only countries that people on the left would rather live in are countries that are significantly less diverse and more white than America. Seems rather hypocritical, doesn't it?

After asking that, it is good to pressure them on their opportunities in America. "What opportunities do you not have in America?" or "What specific laws or regulations target minorities to make it so they can't succeed?" People you talk to will not be able to list any specific laws that target minorities because there are none, so at this point you then ask them if they know the stats on racism we talked about previously, essentially disproving the racist narrative. When they inevitably don't know these facts you present them with, that is a big learning moment for them, and then you can end with the finisher. "If America is such a racist place, why is America the most immigrated-to country in the world by far?" People from all over the world from all different racial backgrounds come to America because they know how great this country is and how much opportunity there is here for anyone to make a great life. Using these questions and the facts discussed previously, you can change people's minds about racism and wake them up to the excellence of America.

In one of the first videos I made, I went to Venice Beach and asked people of all different races about racial identity. I asked black people if they were proud to be black, white people if they were proud to be white, and whether it is right to be proud of your racial heritage. Every single person I talked to was proud of their own race, and they rejoiced with people of other races who were also proud of their heritage. The main through line within that video was that all of these people, despite their race, were proud to be American first and foremost. The mainstream media and the universities will tell you that racism is the biggest issue in America, but in reality, the overwhelming majority of people are completely fine with people of other races and take more pride in being American than anything else. So much for the left's racist narrative.

. . . .

Chapter 2

CORONAVIRUS

THE CORONAVIRUS PANDEMIC has been the most controversial and politically charged issue in recent American history. It has torn families apart, destroyed businesses, and ravaged the mental health of our country. It seems like every person in America has a different opinion on what should be done, who's to blame, and how our country should have handled the virus. I'm sure your mom has a different opinion than your sister, who has a different opinion than your dad, who has a different opinion than your coworker, who has a different opinion than your pastor, who has a different opinion than you. No one can agree on anything when it comes to COVID-19, and it has turned this whole pandemic into a gigantic cluster of conspiracy, fear, and misinformation.

So, what is really going on? How did everything

become so politicized in the first place, and how can you change minds on this issue? Let's get into the most difficult and divisive problem in this book. I'm sure no one will have a problem with anything I have to say in this chapter!

Just to show you guys how incredibly backward this whole thing has gotten, let's start with what I think is the stupidest thing about the restrictions placed on us. Imagine you and your friend are hungry, so you decide to go to a restaurant during the pandemic. You get to the restaurant, and while waiting at the host stand, you have your mask down. The host tells you that you have to wear your mask while waiting, or you won't be seated. You do as they ask and pull your mask up over your nose and mouth. They then guide you to your table while you are still masked and then sit you down nearby someone else. Then once you're sitting down, you can take off your mask. So, I can only get sick or infect someone else if I am at the host stand? Once I am sitting at my table the virus magically disappears and I can't get sick anymore? What a ludicrous practice. Or how about the fact that people weren't allowed to go to church and worship, *even with* social distancing, but you're allowed to go on a plane crammed right next to someone else and take off your mask to eat and drink? Or how about the fact that you weren't allowed to hold a funeral for your loved ones, people who have been integral to your life and done so much for you, but you were allowed to go into a department store and buy a new comforter? None of the lockdown restrictions made any logical sense when all were put next to each other and this only further added to the confusion and anger felt by so many people during this time. If the government was at least consistent with the health standards it wanted to impose, I don't think they would have been met with nearly as much pushback. But because the government mandated the lockdown and restrictions with such inconsistencies, it only set itself up to even more distrust and criticism.

Then along with this, you had the sheep. I'm sure you know the types. I went into the grocery store in the summer of 2020 when the pandemic was in full effect, and I didn't have a mask on. Just as I was walking out of the vegetable section to get in line at the self-checkout, some guy with a mohawk and jean jacket came up to me and started cursing me out. "F%$* you! You d!#&-head!" I had never met this person before in my life, and now he was cursing me out in the produce aisle of a Ralphs, all for not wearing a mask. These are the sheep I am talking about. People who hear what CNN says or what their favorite millionaire celebrity says or what their government says and eat it all up with no questions asked. They want to shame and destroy any person who disagrees with them about Covid and label you a killer and a terrible, horrible person if you don't agree with everything Gavin Newsom and his slicked-back hair have said. These people, along with the government, celebrities, and leftist mainstream media, made this pandemic into what it was: a total and complete shaming of the other side. It wasn't about health or keeping people safe; it was about an agenda and control. And you know the worst part? The ridiculous politicians didn't even follow the guidelines they put in place!

Nothing makes me angrier than a hypocrite. If I disagree with you or you have wrong ideas but you stick by them and don't go back on what you said, I will always respect you more than someone who is a flip-flopper. So, when I see government politicians, *people who are paid by our tax dollars*, breaking the same restrictions that they put in place for us, I get so incredibly frustrated and angry. How can Nancy Pelosi tell us how dangerous the virus is and tell us we always have to wear a mask and shut down businesses and then make a secret hairstylist appointment while the rest of us can't? Or how can Andrew Cuomo keep New York locked down and again tell everyone we always have to wear masks and then get pictured with people not wearing a mask out in public? Or the worst of them, Gavin Newsom, the governor of California, the state with some of the harshest COVID restrictions in the country. During the time when Gavin Newsom had locked down the state and forced businesses and restaurants to remain closed for dine-in, the governor of California decided to go out and get dinner with his friends. They were celebrating another bureaucrat's birthday at the French Laundry, an upscale restaurant in Napa, and they had their own private room where they ate and had no masks on, definitely not practicing social distancing. Rules for thee but not for me, I suppose. Then Gavin Newsom kept his winery open during the lockdown while other wineries and entertainment businesses were forced to close. I don't think there's any other way around it—these people are evil. They impose restrictions on us, destroying our livelihoods, and negatively affecting our mental health, but then they don't even abide by the restrictions they put in place for the rest of us. No wonder nobody trusts politicians; they are all a bunch of hypocrites.

As of January 21, 2021, 643 people have died from COVID who are under the age of 25. All these deaths are sad, but is 643 really that many? I went out on the streets of Hollywood to ask about how many young people have died from the virus, and people's guesses were incredibly far off the mark. Some guessed thousands, others guessed tens of thousands, and all of them were shocked to hear that the number was only in the hundreds. It made them wonder why we even had the restrictions for young people in the first place, like they had been lied to about the severity of the virus. All they heard on the news and on social media is how deadly and terrible COVID-19 was, but when looking at the data, the deaths do not reflect that scenario at all for young people.

Now I know what you're going to say: "But then they give it to old people, and the old people die!" Well, let's look at some data. It is actually very unlikely that young people, particularly students, will transmit the virus to older teachers. A study conducted by scientists at the Institut Pasteur found that there is little data to support the claim that children will infect their teachers or even other students. Out of the 1,340 people who were linked to primary schools included in the study, only 139 of those people were infected, and no one who got it died. They also found that the children who did get infected were not really infected by other children or teachers but by their own parents in the home. Older populations are definitely at a higher risk for contracting and dying from COVID-19, but children and people under the age of 25 are at a very low risk. There was no reason to lock down the schools during the pandemic and ruin children's learning and mental health and social skills, and if we really wanted to do something to help, we should have kept older populations more isolated and let young people go on with their lives.

People always ask about New York City and why there were so many deaths there in the beginning. Well, that is because the state did a horrible job with their older population and keeping them away from infected people. The majority of people who died from COVID-19 in that first wave in New York were older people and nursing home patients, and instead of keeping these people out of harm's way, nursing homes kept infected people at the homes around other old people in the homes. This is how the virus spread so quickly in the older populations there. There were also many flights coming from Wuhan, China, where the virus originated, into Manhattan, an incredibly densely populated place, and people from Wuhan didn't stop coming in until Trump banned travel from China. If New York wanted to put an end to the virus, it should have taken better care of its older population and banned travel from China earlier.

So many things have been politicized with this issue, but the two biggest ones are masks and hydroxychloroquine. In March 2020, at the beginning of the COVID craziness, Dr. Anthony Fauci said on *60 Minutes*, referring to masks, "It's not providing the perfect protection people think that it is." Then a month later all hell broke loose, and all of the bureaucrats changed their mind really quick on masks and said they are absolutely necessary. I'm writing this chapter on a flight to Dallas in January 2021, and there are people on my flight with two or even three masks on at once. If you don't wear a mask, you are seen as the devil to the mask police, and there is no worse thing you can do in America right now than go outside with no mask on. But do the masks even work? Well, according to the *New England Journal of Medicine*, "We know that wearing a mask outside health care facilities offers little, if any, protection from infection. Public health authorities define a significant exposure to Covid-19 as face-to-face contact within 6 feet with a patient with symptomatic Covid-19 that is sustained for at least a few minutes (and some say more than 10 minutes or even 30 minutes). The chance of catching Covid-19 from a passing interaction in a public space is therefore minimal. In many cases, the desire for widespread masking is a reflexive reaction to anxiety over the pandemic." Scientists at the University of Oxford and Bond University found as well that masks had little to no impact on contracting the virus. The study concludes, "Compared to no masks, there was no reduction of influenza-like illness cases or influenza for masks in the general population, nor in healthcare workers." There are plenty of other studies just like these showing the inefficiency of masks. I'm sure you guys reading this know someone who always wears their mask and yet somehow still got infected with the virus. Most scientists and healthcare professionals will say that masks do play a small role in stopping particles from spreading, but the truth of the matter is that masks are not the miracle COVID stopper that you are told they are, and if you don't wear one while you are strolling your local park, you are not killing grandmas all over the world.

Now, I'm not a doctor, and you should always talk to your doctor, but let's talk about HCQ. Hydroxychloroquine has been used as a treatment for years, specifically for lupus and other ailments. Then the COVID pandemic hits, and it is found that it may be a possible treatment for COVID, and everything is all good. Then President Trump comes out on March 21 and says that HCQ might work and be a game changer, and the media loses its mind. It is an immediate switch from "HCQ has some possibility in helping Covid-19 patients" to "HCQ will practically kill you and Trump is a crazy conspiracy theorist."

But does it work? Studies show that HCQ helps zinc get into the cells where the COVID virus replicates, and zinc disrupts the replication of COVID. Some studies show little impact of HCQ being successful but don't include the important adjunct zinc supplement with HCQ. Regardless of what you personally think about HCQ, there are studies and data to show that it may have an impact in treating COVID-19, but none of this mattered to the mainstream media or big tech. Pharmacies refused to dispense HCQ, even though it is proven safe and it is cheap. They let politics interfere with a doctor's freedom to treat patients. It also didn't matter what the doctors said about it.

Here at PragerU, we put out a video sharing what a doctor had to say about HCQ on Twitter, and Twitter decided to suspend our account unless we deleted the video. When it came to HCQ, there was no room for discussion. Big tech had decided that HCQ didn't work and that if you said anything about it your account would be deleted. The effects of HCQ were not up for debate, even among experts and doctors, and if you went against their agenda, you were silenced. When we had a call with Facebook about another video of ours being removed that pertained to HCQ, our chief marketing officer asked, "If someone shared a personal testimony about how they took HCQ and it helped them with their COVID symptoms, would Facebook delete the post?" Facebook said yes. So even if you are posting a public, personal testimony of its results in helping you, you will be silenced. There are countless stories of people who had taken HCQ in conjunction with zinc and had been helped, but big tech wouldn't allow that and would do anything in its power to snuff out dissenting voices. In June, *The Lancet*, considered the world's most prestigious medical journal, was forced to retract a negative study about hydroxychloroquine—talk about the politicization of healthcare.

One of the most vexing problems of this coronavirus pandemic is how deaths are actually classified. It has been shown, even by the CDC, that many of the deaths from COVID were not from COVID after all but from other health conditions while also having COVID. In other words, many people with preexisting conditions who also tested positive for COVID were listed as COVID deaths despite dying from other conditions. We saw this primarily in nursing home patients, where 50 percent of all COVID deaths were recorded. Older people in these homes had conditions before, but when they died and tested positive for COVID, their deaths were listed as COVID deaths. We also saw this in hospitals, where people died from other causes but their deaths were also listed as COVID deaths. Hospitals would even classify deaths from COVID before lab confirmation, and since hospitals got more money from Medicare for a COVID patient, there was a huge incentive for them to list deaths as COVID deaths, even if that wasn't really the case. The numbers for COVID have been heavily manipulated, and I can confidently say at this point that there is probably no one out there who has an accurate grasp on the actual number of people who have died from COVID.

Speaking of deaths and conditions caused by COVID but not actually from COVID, let's look at the negative effects of the lockdowns that took place all over the country. Luckily for me, when the lockdowns started in California, I had amazing friends who weren't too scared of the virus, and I even adopted a dog to keep me company. My business with PragerU was also deemed essential by the government, so I didn't end up working from home for very long. My situation during the lockdowns has been fairly mild, but I have seen lives destroyed of friends and countless others who have contacted me during this time talking to me about how terrible the lockdowns have been for them. I've talked to countless people whose businesses have been destroyed and forced to close, I've talked to therapists who have seen a huge uptick in mental health patients, I've spoken with parents and teachers whose children were losing out on critical social interaction and learning, and I've talked to hundreds of people who are just plain lonely and anxious being stuck at home. During the lockdowns, we have seen the highest suicide rate since the Great Depression. Unemployment has blown up, and people have been turning to substance abuse at a rate higher than ever before. Liquor stores and weed dispensaries were able to stay open and were deemed essential while essential community gatherings such as churches were forced to close, leaving millions of people alone with drugs and alcohol and no communal social interactions. We also have seen millions of patients miss routine screenings for cancer, routine childhood vaccinations, and annual exams. This will lead to thousands of people potentially missing out on lifesaving screenings that would catch illnesses early, and thus more people will die. It seems clear to me when looking at the effects of the lockdown that the solution was worse than the initial problem it was trying to solve.

The whole situation with masks is up for debate, the whole situation with HCQ is up for debate, the whole situation with counting COVID deaths is up for debate, and how well the lockdowns worked is up for debate. But regardless of what you think of all of these issues, there is no debate surrounding the fact that the COVID pandemic and all of its related issues have been incredibly politicized and have bred a huge fear and pessimism for all Americans. I know for a fact that when I'm walking down the street and pass someone, the first thing in both of our minds when we cross paths is *Does this person have COVID?* And this is coming from me, someone who has never been afraid of this virus or been an apocalyptic person. We have been so socialized due to this pandemic to be fearful of other people that we will see the repercussions of this for years to come. You know it's bad when a lady in my apartment complex sees me walking my dog and instead of walking by me with her mask on, she decides to turn around and walk around the parking lot the long way to avoid having to pass me. I am more scared of how people will treat each other in the future and how we move forward in America after this level of fear has been instilled in us—far more than I am afraid of this virus. The main point of changing minds on the issue of COVID and the lockdowns is not to make others think the virus is some sort of hoax or all a conspiracy but to get them to end their fear and open up their minds to people with a different opinion than them. It is also important to focus on the infringements of liberties and freedom we have seen in America during this pandemic and get the person you're talking with to realize the huge negative impacts these lockdowns have had.

In Los Angeles near the PragerU office, there is a restaurant that has been around for years on the famous Ventura Boulevard called Pineapple Hill Saloon. It is the Minnesota Vikings gameday bar for people who live in the valley and has been a huge community meetup place for years and years, but all of that changed with the pandemic. The restaurant was forced to shut down indoor dining first and then, after spending hundreds of dollars on constructing an outside eating area, it had to shut down outdoor dining as well per government orders. This would have been fine if the government's standards for outdoor dining were consistent across the board, but on an afternoon a few days after outdoor dining was closed, it was proven that the government had no sense of what it was doing and the effects. A film crew decided to film right near the Pineapple Hill Saloon. Then when lunchtime came, right outside this restaurant that was forced to shut down outdoor dining, they all set up tables and ate outside. The owner of Pineapple Hill Saloon was furious and sad and overwhelmed, not understanding why this film crew could eat outside in a huge group but she wasn't allowed to serve people at her own restaurant outside. Her business was struggling, her employees were desperate, and her own community had no idea what to do. She filmed a video outside after this happened that went viral, explaining what was going on and the hypocrisy, but despite the millions of people seeing her video, nothing happened. The government still continued its lockdown that was inconsistent and not based on science, the politicians still took money from certain businesses that paid them off to keep their industries open, and the people so afraid of COVID still remained afraid of COVID and nothing changed. This story is a great starting point for a conversation that then leads into your next questions. This story gives a strong ground for the hypocrisy within the government and how the standards of the lockdown didn't make any sense, and it will make whomever you're talking to feel incredible sympathy for the struggling businesses across the country and think about how we can help them.

After talking about Pineapple Hill Saloon, you can go further into the hypocrisy of our politicians and bring up the examples of them breaking their own lockdown rules. "If our politicians really thought this virus was so horrible or wanted to protect us, why are there multiple examples of these politicians breaking their own rules they put in place for us? Doesn't that make you weary about the validity of the lockdowns in the first place if the same people imposing them don't even follow their own rules?" When you get that point to them, they will start to question what their leaders have said to them and whether they are honest. You then can ask more about specifics of the other things that have gone on during the pandemic and their politicization. "Why do you think

HCQ has become such a political subject? Why do you think the masks got so political? Why do you think the stay-at-home order got so political? Why is the severity of the disease such a left versus right issue?" If you can get their answers to these questions and explain to them a new point of view while also making them understand that the people imposing these things are not always to be trusted, you can end on a final question: "People have died from the virus, and it has been a definite pandemic in our country, but do you think all the fear is justified? Do you think people should be fearful and scared of getting back to normal, or should we be hopeful and look at the facts and let people live their lives in a safe and responsible way?" Most rational people will agree with you and want to get the world back to the way it was before 2020. Nobody wants to wear their mask, nobody wants to only order takeout, nobody wants to not visit their dying loved ones, and nobody naturally wants to be afraid. If you convince people that panic has been instilled in them and that all their fear is irrational, you can really make a turnaround in their head. Keep the conversation positive, stay away from rabbit holes of thoughts, and keep it on track, and you can make people not only change their mind on the pandemic but have a better outlook on life and a happier existence, and that is the best possible outcome for everybody.

Chapter 3

. . . .

FREEDOM OF SPEECH

A FEW YEARS AGO, I went on a college speaking tour of the United States. This was meant to be a tour where I went to colleges and expressed to hundreds of students every night the importance of conservative values and the exceptionalism of America. Toward the middle of the tour, I ended up in the great state of Utah.

The first night, I did my usual speech at the University of Utah to a large group of a few hundred students in one of the auditoriums on campus with no problems. The second night, I was slated to speak at a high school in Park City, where the student group Turning Point USA brought me to speak to their chapter of students.

Unfortunately, things didn't go as planned. That afternoon, I got a call from the student who was helping to put on the event. He was the chapter president of the TPUSA group there, and what he said absolutely floored me. Earlier that day, one of the students who wasn't so happy about me coming to campus (a leftist student) had taken matters into their own hands, emptying a can of bear spray into the vents of the auditorium where I was supposed to speak. His little stunt made the air toxic to anyone going inside. One student was poisoned and hospitalized, and 19 others reported difficult breathing and feeling nauseous.

In the end, the event was canceled, all in the name of stopping an evil, racist conservative like me. At other events, I have been protested, I have been canceled, and administrations and students have tried to shut me down, sometimes successfully. At Belmont in Tennessee, I had to move one of my events to an off-campus coffee shop when the administration canceled my event at the last minute, claiming my event would make their campus "unsafe." They did not provide any details about who exactly would be made "unsafe" or how my words would endanger anyone. But I don't think they thought about it all that much.

I'd like you to ponder for a minute and try to think of an event from a left-wing campus speaker that has been shut down by conservative activists. We know this has happened with conservative events. Ben Shapiro has been shut down multiple times. So have Dave Rubin, Ann Coulter, and a long list of other people who have committed the crime of having conservative ideas. But have conservative students ever come and screamed evil, horrible things at the top of their lungs at a left-wing speaker in recent memory? While researching this, I found one example of a couple of MAGA hat–wearing adults yelling at an event in Whittier, California, but that was about it. This is in stark contrast to when conservative speakers have events at college campuses, where, I can speak from experience from many events, one of the biggest costs the students' groups sponsoring the events have to worry about is the massive security cost. It is not rare but expected that leftists on the campus will make some sort of disturbance or try to shut the event down, so security is a must at any conservative event. The people who preach tolerance, love, and acceptance are actually the least accepting, loving, and tolerant people. Who would've guessed?

At the University of California Berkeley, I made a video asking students about free speech. One man told me that since I had a camera, I was "probably a fascist." Another student told me, "If you're making someone feel bad, then you shouldn't be allowed to say it." The left will come and tell you that "hate speech" is not free speech. They will tell you that the speeches I would give on college campuses, or frankly the words in this book, are dangerous and can hurt people. They believe that speech that is considered hateful or dangerous by their standards should be censored and not allowed to be heard. They label people like me or Ben Shapiro or Candace Owens or Dennis Prager as "evil" or "Nazis" to justify them shutting down the things we have to say. If they label the things we say as hateful or evil or dangerous and call the people saying them Nazis, then they feel righteous about shutting us down, like they're performing a moral obligation to protect the world. But it is all a facade, and they know it. They know I'm not a Nazi, and they know I'm not evil; they just don't want a difference of opinion being shared to a large audience, so they shame and ostracize us in an attempt to stifle our dissenting views. The left doesn't actually debate our ideas but our character, oftentimes mischaracterizing us and lying to make sure our "hate speech" is never heard.

Now, I differ from some conservatives when I say that hate speech does exist. Some people go around saying hate speech isn't real with big posters and signs, but I've always known that hate speech is a very real and tangible thing. People say horrible and hateful things all the time, and to say that hate speech doesn't exist is a fault by conservatives trying too hard to be abrasive and aggressive. To win on this front, we have to sympathize with the left and recognize that hate speech is undoubtedly real. The real distinction should not be whether hate speech is real but whether hate speech is legal.

In 1978, neo-Nazis decided that they were going to go marching in Skokie, Illinois, a neighborhood where many Holocaust survivors lived. The local townspeople were not thrilled by this, as you can imagine, and claimed they wanted to live free from intimidation from the neo-Nazi group. The ACLU ended up picking up the neo-Nazis' case and won in court in favor of the neo-Nazis defending their right to march and have freedom of speech. So even Nazis, some of the worst people to ever exist in the world, have the right to come and speak their hateful rhetoric in America. That is how powerful our First Amendment is. But despite allowing us a lot of freedom and expression, America's First Amendment does have certain limitations. You cannot threaten people verbally, and libel, obscenity, and seditious speech are among other examples of speech not protected by the First Amendment. Other than these exceptions, though, it is pretty fair game for you to be able to speak your mind. If you hate fat people with mohawks, you have the absolute right to say out loud that you hate fat people with mohawks. If you are a Nazi and are not threatening anyone with your speech, then in America you have the absolute right to preach your hatred.

Leftists who try to tell you that hate speech should not be allowed aren't just denying you the ability to speak your mind, they are denying you your God-given right of freedom of speech.

The left is in control of the culture, the media, Hollywood, and universities as of now, but what if the left wasn't in control? What if the majority started calling *their* thoughts and opinions hate speech—would they still be for shutting down hate speech then? Herbert Hoover famously said, "It is a paradox that every dictator has climbed to power on the ladder of free speech. Immediately on attaining power each dictator has suppressed all free speech except his own." Every time dictators have taken power throughout history, they have taken away people's ability to speak freely. Our First Amendment isn't just about protecting speech deemed as hateful but about protecting speech that can be used to speak about grievances happening within our own government. The Nazis in Germany, the communists in Russia and China, and various other dictators all around the world took people's free speech away when they rose to power to ensure that their people couldn't rebel. Their speech was censored, propaganda was everywhere, and people were forced to accept the dictator's narrative. On a smaller scale today, this is what is happening with the modern-day left. Big tech companies censor conservative accounts and ideas, people get shamed and have to apologize for having conservative views, and if you support Donald Trump, it could cost you your job or your spot getting into a university. The left is in complete control of the cultural lexicon in America, and they wield their disdain for conservative ideas with an iron fist.

But again, what if the left wasn't in control? It's very easy for them to call conservative speech hateful and say that it shouldn't be uttered while they're in charge, but what if someone else was in charge? Would the left still be all for censoring speech and deeming hate speech not protected if someone else was deciding what the standards for hate speech were? Right now, the left decides the standards for hate speech. If you say there are only two genders, that is hate speech. If you say police violence isn't as big an issue as the media portrays it, that is hate speech. The left decides the narrative, and thus, they decide what constitutes hate speech and what doesn't, but I can guarantee you if the roles were reversed and the other side started calling their leftist views hate speech, they would be screaming for the First Amendment and saying that their rights were being taken away. That is why our First Amendment is so important: because it protects the minority. No matter how unpopular your views, no matter who is in charge of the country or the culture, you have the God-given right to speak your mind freely without fear of suppression.

No other country has a First Amendment like America does. Other countries have their own brand of "freedom of speech," but no country has freedom of speech like the United States of America. When our Founding Fathers created this country and created the Bill of Rights, they knew that American citizens didn't get their rights within it from them; they knew they got these rights from God. There is no other constitution in the world that was created like that, and America's First Amendment is written in such a way as to give more power to citizens than any other country in the world. In the UK, hate speech laws punish you if you say something hateful toward another person or group, which we have seen in full effect with people getting arrested and even jailed for their comments made on social media. The same holds true in many other countries the left would claim are as free as America, such as Canada, Australia, and France. As police in these countries continue to monitor "hateful" comments on social media, crime is on the rise within. At least they're stopping all those mean Twitter comments, though, right?

When the government controls what speech is considered hateful and what is not, then you are at risk of oppression or, worse, tyranny. In the United Kingdom in 2016, a man named Mark Meechan, going by the name of Count Dankula on social media, posted a video of his pug acting like a Nazi. He said, "My girlfriend is always ranting and raving about how cute and adorable her wee dog is so I thought I would turn him into the least cute thing I could think of, which is a Nazi." He made a joke online, posted it, and thought nothing of it, but the UK police had a different reaction. Meechan was arrested for the video in 2018 for breaching the Communications Act of 2003. After being tried and found guilty, he had to pay 800 pounds for the Nazi pug joke he made. Of course, the video he made could be deemed offensive, it could be in bad taste, and it could even be hurtful to a lot of people, but the problem isn't whether you think he should have made the video or whether it was funny but whether he should be allowed to make the comment. There are social implications for all of our speech, of course, but that is completely separate from any legal ramifications the government can put on you for saying it, and this is just one of countless examples of other countries not supporting an individual's right to speak their mind freely.

Big tech censorship is a whole nother animal. YouTube, Google, and other big tech platforms say they are platforms where anyone can come and express their ideas. YouTube claims that it is "committed to foster-ing a community where everyone's voice can be heard." These platforms claim to protect free speech and indi-viduals' right to speak their minds, but in reality, they're all a gang of liars. Big tech companies censor conserva-tive ideas and voices, including PragerU. PragerU sued YouTube for placing over 50 of its videos on its restricted video list. YouTube claims to restrict videos that are por-nographic, mature, or violent, and somehow PragerU videos, according to YouTube, fall under this category. Who knew a video titled "Why did America fight in the Korean War?" was pornographic? Could have fooled me, PragerU!

In October 2020, a month before Joe Biden was elected president, the *New York Post* ran a story about Hunter Biden and Joe Biden's alleged corruption. The story started going viral, and many prominent figures on social media started sharing the article. Then, out of nowhere, Twitter censored the article and removed the *New York Post*'s Twitter account. The story the *New York Post* shared exposed emails from Hunter Biden and Joe Biden in which Joe Biden was recommending withhold-ing $1 billion in aid to Ukraine when he was vice presi-dent until their government fired a prosecutor who was investigating Burisma, a company whose board Hunter Biden served on. In case you are reading this and don't understand already, this is a huge deal. Not just the story that the *New York Post* reported but the fact that Twitter censored the article and suspended the account of the *New York Post* for posting it. Senator Ted Cruz remarked on this, saying, "If Twitter did not prevent *Buzzfeed* from sharing its reporting on the Steele dossier or the *New York Times* from reporting on President Trump's tax returns, please explain a politically neutral principle for why the reporting is treated differently." This move by Twitter to delete the *New York Post*'s account and the article posted is not just preventing people from having all the information before a major presidential election but is clearly biased censorship toward conservatives. If Republicans and conservatives don't stand up to big tech companies and their clear leftist agenda, our republic will be truly lost. It is one thing to have some leftist on your campus try to tell you supporting President Trump is hateful. It is a whole other beast entirely when some of the largest companies in the world apparently interfere with our elections and stifle the press and millions of people's ability to speak their minds and showcase the truth. Fighting against big tech censorship has to be our biggest battle.

So how do we win against people who believe hateful speech should be censored and that people with conservative views are evil or Nazis? It all starts with the questions, but I want to bring up one thing first. Some people's minds aren't able to be changed. It's a tough fact of life, but some people are incredibly dogmatic about their views, or they don't have an open mind, or they have been told the same things over and over again so many times that they will just not listen to you. I make my videos and interview people and know that this is sometimes the case, but it doesn't deter me from talking to people nonetheless. I may not change the mind of the person I'm talking to, but I will always change the minds of people watching, whether that is in person or once the video is released. With the way I ask questions and the way they answer them, people watching from the outside can still have incredible teaching moments, so it's always important to maintain your composure and debate with integrity in any situation because you never know who is watching. You may not change the mind of the person you're talking to, but there is always opportunity to change the mind of someone watching.

Aside from that, most people are pretty open to new ideas if you ask them the *right* questions in the *right* way. When it comes to freedom of speech, the first question I like to ask to get the conversation going is simple: "What is hate speech?" In an interview I did in Playa Vista, California, asking people about hate speech, I started every interview with this question to get a standing on what they believed about it. One girl in particular said it was anything that someone deems as hateful and that it shouldn't be allowed. I then proceeded to tell her that the answer she just gave was offensive to me and that I don't think she should be allowed to say it. This confused her at first, but then she understood. I had then deemed what she said to me as hateful, and by her logic, what she said shouldn't be allowed. This was a huge learning moment for her in which she came to the realization that anyone could decide something is hateful and thus justify its censorship. I continued to press her and asked her, "Who should decide what is hate speech and what isn't?" She didn't have an answer for that, and I concluded the interview by telling her that when someone decides what is and what isn't deemed hate speech, any opinion you may have that is different from the mainstream could be judged as hateful by whoever sets the rules. She left the interview agreeing with me that hate speech should be allowed and that someone shouldn't have the authority to decide what is and what isn't free speech.

"Should hate speech be censored?" "Who decides what hate speech is and isn't?" and "What if the people in charge decided your opinions were hate speech and tried to silence you? Wouldn't you want the ability to speak out against it?" are the building-block questions to changing minds on this topic. You can eventually go into more detail with listeners, explaining how big tech is censoring us and how tyrannical regimes throughout history have always taken away people's freedom of speech, really driving the point home of how important it is that our speech is never limited. The right to speak freely despite how unpopular your opinion may be is one of the landmarks of what America was founded on, and the people trying to take that ability away from you have to be dealt with. With this guide, you can convince the people around you of the importance of a society that allows its citizens to speak freely. If you are being respectful and offend them with your questioning, do not feel bad or retract your statement. It is far more important to stand by your morals and beliefs than it is to make sure that you never offend a person with a differing view.

Chapter 4

· · · · · · · · · · ·

GUNS AND THE SECOND AMENDMENT

'M GOING TO BE honest with you guys: the issue of what we should do with guns in America is easily one of the hardest topics to change people's minds on. People hear the word *gun* or *rifle*, and their mind automatically goes to the worst atrocities of gun violence in recent years. Sandy Hook, the Las Vegas concert shooting, and the Parkland school shooting were all horrible tragedies that are brought up anytime you try to talk to people about the Second Amendment. All of these mass shootings were incredibly destructive to the communities they took place in and were covered heavily by the media on all sides, giving millions of people strong emotional ties to them. When people see so much death and see that guns were the means of bringing about that carnage, their minds are practically already made up at that point. The key to changing minds on the issue of guns and the Second Amendment is not to downplay any of these shootings or disregard people's concerns over them but to acknowledge the violence and evil within them to make the best case possible for people's freedom to defend themselves from that evil, whether that be from a criminal in your home, a mass shooter, or your own government.

Many on the left believe that if guns were banned, the world would be a much safer place. After the Parkland shooting in February 2018, where 17 people were killed at Marjory Stoneman Douglas High School by a brutal former student, many of the kids at the school helped start the organization March for Our Lives. This organization aimed at bringing about legislation to stop gun violence and making young people's voices heard concerning the Second Amendment. The group held marches and demonstrations across the country where thousands of young Americans rallied and yelled for gun reform as loudly as they could, and I happened to go to the March for Our Lives that took place in Los Angeles that same year. It's important to note that at this point in my career I was still a newbie on the street, and I would go to these marches expecting a level of normalcy. But, of course, I was completely shocked once I got there and saw what the people there were *actually* advocating for. Aside from devolving into a total anti-Trump march and hearing a man tell me we should "melt the guns down and feed them to the homeless," the march was essentially an anti–Second Amendment march. Most people rallying that day weren't advocating for gun safety or a small amount of gun reform. They were advocating for the abolition of the Second Amendment. One girl even had a rally sign with a Second Amendment imprint and a big red X over it. Radical leftist celebrities and politicians will tell you that "they don't want to take your guns away," but when it comes to the actual activists and Democratic supporters, their message is clear and concise. They want an America with no guns and an America with no Second Amendment.

But what's so important about the Second Amendment anyway? To the left, all it is is some protection to give people the right to get guns to shoot up schools and movie theaters. But to the Founding Fathers, it was a necessary protection against a tyrannical government. After the 2008 landmark Supreme Court case *District of Columbia v. Heller,* which dealt with the right to own a handgun, the late Justice Antonin Scalia said, "Undoubtedly some think that the Second Amendment is outmoded in a society where our standing army is the pride of our nation, where well-trained police forces provide personal security, and where gun violence is a serious problem. That is perhaps debatable, but what is not debatable is that it is not the role of this court to pronounce the Second Amendment extinct." Scalia knew that the Second Amendment, along with the other protections endowed to us in the Bill of Rights, was not to be changed because of its importance to the integrity of America. The Second Amendment was not created by the founders to give American citizens a gun for hunting or even just for self-protection. It was created to give every citizen the right to defend themselves from tyranny.

"Americans have the right and advantage of being armed—unlike the citizens of other countries whose governments are afraid to trust the people with arms," our Founding Father James Madison said. When you bring the point up to leftists about tyrannical governments taking away our rights or, even worse, killing their own people, the usual response is a scoff or an "our government is never going to come and just kill people—are you crazy?" But if we take a trip down memory lane, we will see that the historical record paints a much different picture. In 1911, Turkey disarmed its citizens, and from 1915 to 1917 it killed 1.5 million Armenians. In 1929, Russia disarmed its citizens, and it killed over 20 million people over the next 30 years. China disarmed its people in 1935 and killed over 20 million of its own citizens. Germany disarmed its citizens and committed the Holocaust, murdering over 6 million Jews. In 1956, Cambodia disarmed its citizens and ended up killing 1 million people. Between 1964 and 1981, after disarming its citizens, Guatemala murdered over 100,000 Mayans. In 1970, Uganda took guns away from its citizens, and from 1971 to 1979 it killed over 300,000 Christians. And this list of atrocities is only a partial account of people murdered by tyrannical governments after their right to arms was stripped away. The left laughs and snickers at conservatives when we show our fear for overreaching governments taking control and murdering their people, but when you look at what has happened to countries and people throughout history who *have* lost the right to bear arms, you can clearly see that it is the last thing we should be scoffing at. The Second Amendment in America protects us from such tyranny by giving us the ability to defend ourselves from a government that gained total dominion over us. Just like our First Amendment, no other country in the world has a Second Amendment like we do in America, and this amendment within the Bill of Rights ensures that all of our other rights are kept.

Aside from the Second Amendment being the great equalizer to stop a tyrannical government, it also provides American citizens the ability to defend themselves from evil on all fronts. When I was growing up in Colorado, one of my favorite movie theaters to go to was the Century 16 theater in Aurora. It wasn't the nicest theater, and it wasn't in a great part of town, but it was close, and the tickets were cheap so my mom and I went there throughout my childhood to see all sorts of new films. But after my freshman year of high school, we couldn't go to that movie theater anymore. We didn't want to go to that movie theater anymore. On July 20, 2012, a man came to the movie theater during a showing of *The Dark Knight Rises* and brutally gunned down the people enjoying the midnight showing. Twelve people were killed, and 70 were injured, some of them being friends I knew from high school. No one in the movie theater had a gun to stop the shooter, there was no armed security guard to stop him, and by the time the police got there, the damage had already been done. It was an incredibly tragic event for our community and was breaking news on every TV station for numerous days after it happened.

Now let's compare this to the shooting, or should I say attempted mass shooting, at a church in White Settlement, Texas, in December 2019. The shooter, identified now as Keith Kinnunen, opened fire at the West Freeway Church of Christ, killing two people before being shot by a member of the church's volunteer armed security team. The shooter was ready to kill many members of the church but was stopped by the good guy with a gun, a concept the left claims doesn't exist. The volunteer security guard at the church, Jack Wilson, saved potentially dozens of lives that day, all because he had the proper training and was in the right place at the right time with his own firearm.

I made a video asking students at Pasadena Community College about the concept of a good guy with a gun, and the answers I received to my questions were just as expected from people at a California university. "Good guys with guns don't exist." "No one should have a gun." Even "I don't need a gun because I'm a nice person." That's right, because criminals with guns only rob and kill mean people—that makes sense. But regardless of the answers they gave me when the conversation started, I was able to change the mind of everyone I talked to by the end with some pretty simple logic: "If a criminal had two options: (a) Shoot people in a building where no one had a gun to defend themselves or (b) shoot people in a building where people are armed and trained to defend themselves, which place would that criminal choose to go and commit his crime?" Saying this question out loud or just thinking about it for over a second, the answer becomes incredibly obvious, but it is shocking to see just how many people have never thought about it this way. This question, along with the fact that 98 percent of mass shootings happen in gun-free zones, is a fantastic way to help convince people of the necessity of armed people to equal out the playing field against evil. If they're still not convinced after that or they just want to know more, there is a lot more you can get into, specifically how people handle guns for self-protection in this country. Every single year in America, guns are used defensively 500,000 to 3 million times. That is *a lot* of people defending themselves using a firearm. Just imagine if these people didn't have a firearm to defend their homes, their loved ones, and themselves. How much more senseless violence would have occurred without these people having the God-given rights of the Second Amendment?

But what actually happens when we restrict people's access to guns? Have we done that in America? The short answer is no. The long answer is that there are certain cities across the country with very heavy gun regulations that make it very tedious and difficult for everyday Americans to own a firearm. One of these cities is Chicago. Chicago has some of the strictest gun laws in the country and also one of the highest yearly numbers of gun deaths. This is no coincidence. Chicago mayor Lori Lightfoot will tell you these gun deaths are from guns purchased across state lines and that Chicago's strict gun regulations would work if it weren't for these conservative states with lax gun laws, but I believe that is a total lie. Most guns used by criminals are stolen or bought illegally, which means citizens who can't purchase guns easily and legally are left defenseless against criminals who get their guns illegally. Most criminals getting their guns illegally means that the vast majority of Americans with legally purchased firearms aren't committing crimes and are living in accordance with the law. In fact, concealed carry permit holders are some of the most law-abiding citizens in the country. Over roughly the past 15 years there have been over 18 million concealed carry permit holders who have in total committed 801 firearm homicides during those 15 years. This means concealed carry permit holders are responsible for 0.7 percent of all murders involving guns, and when looking at the data, they are even more well-behaved than members of law enforcement. Safe gun owners with proper gun training are the best equalizer to stopping criminals with illegally acquired guns, so when you take away people's ability to be safe and responsible gun owners, like in Chicago, you are only opening up your city for more and more death.

Let's look at some modern examples of what happens when you take guns away from your citizens and the implications of that, specifically in the United Kingdom. In the UK, 59 percent of burglaries are hot burglaries, meaning the person is home while the burglary occurs, compared to 13 percent in the United States. Why is that? Well, UK citizens aren't allowed to have guns for self-protection like in the United States, so a criminal with an illegal firearm doesn't face the same risk of dying while breaking into someone's home while someone is there. Knife crime has risen 51 percent since 2011 in the UK, and acid attacks have risen over 74 percent from 2015–2016. As the UK cuts police funding and limits its own citizens' rights to defend themselves from these violent criminals, crime continues to rise. This data also means that as guns are less available for people, criminals will still find a way to commit crimes, whether that be with knives, hands, or acid. This has contributed to London having a higher murder rate than New York City in 2018, a figure never before seen in modern history. The data seems pretty clear about what happens when you take away people's guns. Criminals still find a way to use the illegal ones to commit crimes, and now citizens have no way to defend themselves. The left thinks they're doing something virtuous by taking away people's firearms, but really all they're doing is opening them up to even more violence and evil.

But what about the left's concerns with these so-called "weapons of war" we hear so much about? This question gets us into some of the best questions to ask the person whose mind you're trying to change. Many rational people on the left when asked about guns will say they are fine with someone having a gun at home to defend their family, like a dad having a handgun, but are against these "assault weapons" that are murdering thousands of people every year. This is a great starting point. Ask them if they are fine with someone having a handgun to defend themselves and then transition to the "assault-style weapons," which they will inevitably want to ban. Then it is important to ask them to define what an assault weapon is in the first place. Most won't have a good answer, so you can rebut by telling them the fact that automatic weapons are banned from civilian purchase in this country. Then ask them if they mean things like AR-15s. They will say yes, and then it's time to get into the facts about firearm deaths in this country. In 2017, 64 percent of all gun-related deaths were due to handguns. Two percent were attributed to shotguns and 4 percent to rifles, which includes those big and scary AR-15s. The other 30 percent are unidentified, but it can be assumed that many more of those deaths are also from handguns. The vast majority of murders by guns in this country are committed with handguns, yet most people will tell you that those are okay, but the rifles are not. After explaining to them the facts about the handgun deaths in this country, ask them this question: "If handguns kill 16 times more people than rifles in this country every year, wouldn't you want to ban handguns instead of rifles?" This puts them in a quandary where they are forced to reevaluate their position on the types of guns they would want to ban. You then bring up the facts we discussed earlier concerning how legal gun owners use guns defensively every year to protect themselves, and at this point you should be at the tipping point of changing their mind. To finish, you can end with this: "Politicians and celebrities on TV advocate against guns and people's rights to have them, yet they have armed security with guns to defend them with. Seems rather hypocritical, doesn't it?"

Chapter 5

....

ILLEGAL
IMMIGRATION

WHEN I FIRST moved to Hollywood, California, I was a 20-year-old single guy. I went on dates with some different girls I met but never found any I really vibed with all that well. Eventually I ended up going on a date with this cute girl who went to USC, and for the most part, we had a nice night. We went and saw the views in the Hollywood Hills and got some pizza, and then she was going to take me back to my place. (And, yes, *she* was driving for our first date. Breaking gender dating norms. I was so progressive back then!) We pulled up to my spot, and before I left, we started talking about what we did for a living, which somehow hadn't come up on our date thus far. She told me what she was doing at USC, and I can't remember now what it was exactly, but I think it was some social justice prelaw path or something just as ridiculous. Then she asked what I did. At this point in my life, I had recently dropped out of college and moved to Los Angeles to intern for PragerU, so I told her I worked in politics. Her face scrunched, and I could tell she was curious.

"Politics? Like what kind of politics?" she asked. I told her straight up, "Conservative politics," and her curious face turned into more of a grimace. "What, so did you, like, vote for Trump?" she probed in the most typical LA girl way of asking things. Without hesitation, I answered back, "Hell yeah I did. Love that guy!" At this point she stopped talking and looked away, just staring out the front window. This went on for at least 10 seconds, and it was getting pretty awkward. She finally spoke after what felt like an eternity. "I can't believe I just went on a date with someone who voted for Trump." And then it happened. She started crying. And not just a few tears either—this girl was full-on sobbing in the seat next to me over the fact she just went on a date with an evil, racist Trump supporter. I was absolutely floored at what was happening at this point, and at that moment in time I was just trying to find a way to get out of this car and back into my place. "Are you okay?" I asked her. She turned to me, weeping, with tears rolling down her cheeks, and then she said something I will never forget. "How could you vote for him? *He's going to deport all the immigrants.*" I looked back at her, trying to hold in my laughter at this point, and told her, "Yes, the illegal ones. And he's going to build the wall. It's awesome!" This made her cry even harder, and after that I opened the car door, told her, "Peace out," and left. Thinking back now, I wish I would have said something better than "It's awesome" and had a stronger closing line, but alas, that was the best I could come up with. As you can expect, this girl and I didn't end up working out, and legend has it you can still hear her crying, weeping around the USC campus whenever Trump's wall is mentioned in her presence.

I bring up this story not to just make fun of this girl but to show you how emotional some of these political issues we talk about in this book can be to the left. When it comes to the topic of illegal immigration, leftists have a hard time disconnecting their emotions from the actual solutions for the issue. I believe that on this issue, in contrast to some issues like free speech or racism, the intentions of many leftists are good. They want to help people from other countries who don't have the same opportunities and see that if they come to America, legally or illegally, they will be better off. While it is true that people coming to this country will most likely have a better life than they would live anywhere else, that still doesn't mean we should support their illegal entry here. Illegal immigration costs our country billions of dollars every year, invites crime to this country, and breeds an unfair system where people get benefits in this country that they didn't equally pay into in the first place.

Many on the left are pro–illegal immigration and actively advocate for people coming to this country illegally and the ending of all deportations. They are against any sort of wall to keep people out on the Mexican border, and many of them want the U.S. Immigration and Customs Enforcement (ICE) disbanded. They shame American leaders who want to deport illegal aliens in America or who want to end sanctuary cities. They believe it is immoral to not let people into this country and think that if you are against illegal immigration, you are a racist who obviously hates Mexicans. But the truth is, there is nothing hateful about wanting to keep people out who want to come here illegally. In fact, I would argue that wanting to stop illegal immigration is the least racist position you can take on the issue, and here's why.

In chapter 1, we talked about racism and how economic and cultural issues are the main issues facing the black community, not racist institutions. But one thing we didn't talk about regarding the economic mobility of black people in this country is the effect that illegal immigration has on their opportunities. One in seven working people in America are immigrants, and of that seventh, roughly a third of them are illegal immigrants. As more and more illegal aliens come into America, we see a large spike in the supply of unskilled laborers. Most people coming here illegally aren't doctors or rocket scientists or highly skilled laborers; they are mostly low-skilled, low-wage laborers. Of course, that isn't always the case, but it is the majority. In America, 6 out of 10 black men have a high school degree or less, and thus many of them are only qualified to work in a low-skill job. As illegal immigrants come into this country by the thousands, they take those low-skill jobs and do them for cheaper, thus taking away black men's opportunity in America to get a job and advance themselves. In 2008, the U.S. Commission on Civil Rights presented a study to the president of the United States from top economic experts speaking on how illegal immigration negatively affects the black community in America. Although this study today would be deemed incredibly politically incorrect, the factual evidence provided within still holds true. Dr. Gordon Hanson specifically found in this study that when there is a 10 percent increase in available immigrant labor in the American workforce, there is a 4 percent decrease in black wages and a 3.5 percent decrease in black employment. Lower wages mean many black men look to crime for their income instead of a traditional job when the traditional employment can no longer support them as a result of the immigration influx. Illegal immigration is of course not the only reason for black people in America having shortcomings economically, but it does play a massive role in an already-disappearing low-skill job market. As American companies continue to export factory and manufacturing jobs overseas and leftists do nothing to curb illegal immigration, blacks with already-limited opportunities in America are shafted and left with little chance to find a good job that will give them the ability to provide for themselves. The data is clear—if you care about black lives and helping black people in America, then you have to stand against illegal immigration.

Two hundred billion dollars is paid out every year by taxpayers for illegal immigrants. Not only are illegal immigrants taking many jobs away from low-income communities, but they cost every American a part of their paycheck, to pay for the benefits they receive. This isn't to say illegal immigrants aren't paying any taxes— they are when you look at sales tax and some payroll taxes—but every single American citizen is financially burdened by the impact of having millions of illegal immigrants living here. In 2017 it was recorded that there were over 41,000 illegal immigrants in the federal prison system, and over half of those had been approved for deportation. Each illegal immigrant inmate costs roughly $29,226 per year, which amasses a total of $1.2 billion per year for American taxpayers to shell out. That is all without taking into account the intangible cost of the crimes that these illegal immigrants committed. I do think it's important to make it clear that I am not trying to demonize these immigrants. There are thousands of American citizens every year who also commit horrible crimes and cost our country billions in taxes for their incarceration and punishments, but the difference is exactly that. They *are* American citizens. They pay into our tax system fully, they were born here in this country, and they are the people we should be most worried about. With thousands of American citizens committing crimes in this country already, the last thing we should be worried about is a surplus of people coming in and committing crimes here who didn't have a right to be here in the first place. That only seems fair to me.

There are American citizens struggling all across this country. There are veterans who can't get proper healthcare and treatment, there are thousands of homeless people across the nation with no home or food, and there are thousands of people on food stamps struggling every day just to get by. Shouldn't we as a country be worried about American citizens struggling first and foremost before people who illegally entered this country? Of course, we should feel empathy for people from other countries who have limited opportunities, are trying to escape poverty and war, or are just looking for a better life, but that should come second to the plight of people who were born in this country. American citizens should be at the forefront of whom we are looking to help, but the left insists on their virtue-signaling antics, leaving American-born citizens in the dirt. In my home state of California, we pay millions of dollars in taxes for illegal immigrants every year. California taxpayers pay on average $23.5 billion a year in taxes for illegal immigrants, a $4.7 billion increase since 2010. This includes costs for education, healthcare, and law enforcement and social services, which average a total cost of $2,370 per California household every year. Imagine what a struggling California household could do with an extra $2,370 every year. That could be the difference between a new car to get to work, meals for their family, or even the ability to move to a new state with better policies.

Despite California being one of the worst offenders on this issue, the rest of the nation doesn't fare much better. According to a 2016 study, it costs American public schools $59.8 billion annually to educate the children of illegal immigrants, where over 98 percent of that burden is paid for by state and local taxpayers through property taxes. In terms of healthcare, American taxpayers end up paying roughly $11.9 billion yearly for illegal immigrants. That's $4.6 billion in health services from federal taxes, $2.8 billion in health services from state and local taxes, $3 billion through cost shifting to pay off the debts of uninsured patients, and another $1.5 billion in physician charity care. Then we have ICE spending $4.7 billion annually, where the number of border patrol agents has nearly doubled from 2003 to 2018, and we have a recipe for American citizens paying a whole lot of money for illegal immigrants. Again, I understand why people would want to come here—we are the greatest country in the world with more opportunity than anywhere else—but we have to think of America first. If we really want to help these people, we need to get an easier path to citizenship for them, disincentivize them coming here for unearned benefits, and give them opportunities that don't directly compete with the American citizens born and raised here.

I went to a March for Open Borders—yes, you heard that right, a March for Open Borders—in Los Angeles in 2018, and the majority of the people there were vehemently anti-ICE. They believed it was a terrorist organization, killing poor immigrants and locking children in cages, and many of the protestors' signs said as much. But these people have been fed a lie about the brave men and women in ICE who are helping keep our country safe and secure. When looking at 2019, we can see some of the amazing work ICE has accomplished. People on the left and the right will both agree that human trafficking should be ended immediately, but only the right supports ICE, an organization that puts the end of human trafficking at the forefront of its duty. In 2019, ICE put forth 1,024 human trafficking–related cases that led to 2,197 arrests. This resulted in the saving of over 400 victims of human trafficking and 700 convictions. If the left cares about stopping human trafficking and about children, they will support ICE, an organization dedicated to helping children's lives.

Changing minds on this issue can be difficult. You can give people all the facts and information about the costs and damage that illegal immigration can cause, and they will still be very resistant to changing their mind. Despite all the negative impacts illegal immigration can have on our country, they will often say, "But we have to treat these people fairly. I still think they should be allowed to come here for a better life despite all of that information." It is a fair stance for them to have as well. Even though illegal immigration costs our country $200 billion a year, that doesn't matter if we are helping these people lead productive lives free from poverty and war, according to the left. The most productive way to change minds in this situation is to point out the hypocrisy. Asking them about whether other countries should provide for illegal immigrants is a great place to start. "Do you think you have the right to go into another country—say, Mexico—and get benefits from the government such as free healthcare and free education for your children without paying into the system or being a citizen of Mexico?" The answer is obviously no. The hypocrisy of the left is that they are totally fine with people coming into America and reaping the benefits of being here, but when it comes to any other country, they are totally against it. This isn't because they have never thought about this question either. It is because the left hates America. They don't care about what happens to the economy or the citizens of their country as long as they can morally posture as if they really care about illegal immigrants. If they loved this country, they wouldn't be trying to radically transform it by letting millions of people into it illegally.

Chapter 6

. . . .

FAMILY VALUES

WE DISRUPT THE Western-prescribed nuclear family structure requirement by supporting each other as extended families and 'villages' that collectively care for one another, especially our children, to the degree that mothers, parents, and children are comfortable." This was taken straight from the Black Lives Matter website, that is, until the organization was called out on it and took it down to hide its true intentions. Aside from this making absolutely no sense (what is a "village"?), you can see clearly in the first line that Black Lives Matter wants to disrupt, if not disband, the western nuclear family. And this isn't just within Black Lives Matter; in many sects of leftist thought throughout America, the American nuclear family is a tool of the patriarchy that keeps women down and should be destroyed. As discussed in our chapter about racism, it should come as no surprise that the left wants to keep families apart with no central structure, keeping fathers away from their children, single mothers on welfare, and all parts of the family hooked on government assistance. This is all part of the plan to keep Americans hooked on the Democrat plantation forever.

I grew up without my dad, and for lack of a better descriptor, my dad did some horrible shit. He was in prison while I was growing up, and so the central father figure in my life was never there to teach me how to be a man. I grew up with my mom and sister primarily, and my mom now had on her shoulders the responsibility of turning a young boy who had just gone through horrible and terrible circumstances with his own father into a responsible young man. Luckily for me, she did a great job. I love my mom like nothing else for taking such a vested interest in raising me and teaching me so many valuable lessons, but I was lucky to have a mom who loved and cared for me so much. My mom would work 16-hour shifts nursing on the weekends, and my sister and I were sent to our grandparents' house to learn even more lessons about growing up. My grandparents took us to church, which I absolutely hated as a young kid because I didn't understand it at all, and my grandpa put me into Boy Scouts, which gave me even more of a support system. I also had my older half brother, who I looked up to more than anyone and who taught me even more about growing up. With all of these support systems, I was able to be all right in my life and learn the character and life skills that have made me into the responsible man I am now, but a lot of people aren't so lucky.

Black Lives Matter looking to get rid of the western nuclear family is probably the worst value it has espoused. To me, this is worse than rioting and looting, this is worse than the forced diversity standards it pushes for, and this is worse than their anti-police rhetoric. Family is everything. Children learn their values from their family, they learn how to grow up from their family, and they learn how to be responsible and live as an adult in the real world from their family. Growing up with two married parents in the home is the paramount standard for determining a child's success in America, and the fact that many on the left want to disrupt this structure is truly evil. It shows beyond a shadow of a doubt that they don't care about children in this country and only look to advance their own agenda. No nuclear family means people depend more on the government, and it means children depend more on their teachers and schooling to teach them information and values they're not getting at home. Parents depend on the government and don't learn personal responsibility to teach to their children, kids learn left-ist nonsense from their schools and teachers, and thus you have the recipe for a continuous system that traps millions of Americans in a never-ending cycle of control and poverty. Conservatives could elect the perfect conservative president, who does everything right and has the support of Congress, but none of it matters if families are not together. In a matter of years after that perfect president is out of office, our country will be lost again if our next generation is not educated or brought up in a culture that appreciates the value of the family. Bringing back traditional family values should be at the forefront of the issues that conservatives are pushing for because if we don't, I promise you there will be no chance of ever taking this country back from the grips of leftism.

First, let's take a deeper dive into the results of having an America less focused on the family. According to data from the Heritage Foundation, we can clearly see these adverse effects. A 10 percent increase in the percentage of children living in homes with single parents leads to a 17 percent increase in juvenile crime, and higher-crime neighborhoods are oftentimes accompanied by higher rates of single-parent families. When children don't have love from family members and struggle due to the economic realities of growing up in a single-parent household, they are far more likely to become involved in crime and lead troubled lives. This of course doesn't happen with all children who grow up in single-parent households, but those are anomalies. In 1970, 88 percent of children grew up in two-parent households. Today that number is down to 70 percent. As America continues to disincentivize marriage, we see long-term effects not on just the adults in that situation economically and happiness wise but on the children to an even greater degree.

But the left claims that this is all in the name of disbanding the evil patriarchy. Women don't need to get married or be tied down to kids to be happy; that is only a sexist facade men have promoted for generations. Families are overrated according to the progressive left, and women will be better off having a career and never having children. And I know, I know, I'm not supposed to talk about this because I don't have a uterus, but don't listen to me—let's just look at the data. Using the data from the General Social Survey over the past 35 years, we have seen an overall decline in women's happiness. It's surprising, though, isn't it? The gender pay gap has disappeared, women are more educated than ever (even more than men overall), they no longer have to stay home and be so domestic, and they are free to pursue ventures and careers that they choose. You would think all this freedom for women would result in an over-all gain in happiness for women, right? What is most surprising to me is how in the 1970s women weren't just happier than they are now, they were reported as happier than most men. Now that trend is the oppo-site, where men are shown to be happier than women overall. But is this all correlation without causation? Is this all a coincidence? Many people on the left will tell you it is, but let's look at a very important fact. Data shows that when you are happy, you are more likely to get married than someone who is unhappy. So as the left and progressive feminism have pushed for women to not have children and solely focus on their careers, at the same time, women have become more and more unhappy. Women remain unmarried, as we have seen with declining marriage rates across America. It would seem that as women become unhappier, women also don't get married. Birth rates in America are at the lowest level we have seen in 35 years, but hey, at least women can now have a career and work for their entire lives single and alone, right? Progress!

Look, I have no problem with women having careers alongside men. But it is a lie to say women will be hap-pier if they don't have a family and remain single and childless. And the same is true for men. Both men and women should be getting married and going through life together as partners to make both people happiest and have the best future for America. Although men and women are similar in that way, men and women are different in a lot of other significant ways. I did a video on Hollywood Boulevard asking people what the difference was between men and women, and many of them believed there was no difference other than their private parts. They believed men and women want to have the same careers and get the same fulfillment in their lives and that society has told them that women want different things, but in reality, they are exactly the same. This couldn't be further from the truth. Instead of accepting the biological facts that men and women have different strengths and weaknesses and prioritize different careers and events in their lives, the left wants to tell you they are exactly the same and want the same things out of life. Let's look at Scandinavia. Denmark, a society that pushes incredibly hard for equality between the two genders, still has a 20:1 ratio of female to male nurses. As the society pushes men and women to disband gender norms and institutes affirmative action policies in hiring, females still choose to become nurses, a job that has historically been dominated by women. Men and women have different strengths and are biologically built differently, and thus when left to their own devices in a society focused on equality, they still choose certain careers that reflect those strengths and wants.

These declining marriage rates, the lack of emphasis on family values, and the fact that parents let their children stare at screens all day are also affecting the kids heavily in all of these families. Looking at suicide rates of adolescents in America, we have seen a sharp increase in recent years. The suicide rate for young boys rose 74 percent since 1999, while the suicide rate for young girls rose over 240 percent. These are unprecedented numbers. It is difficult to pinpoint exact reasons for each individual case of suicide, but in America today we have a divorce rate of 40 percent. In 1970, 84 percent of children lived with both of their married biological parents, whereas in 2006 this was only 60 percent. As parents continue to split up, children feel the effects of this and their mental health declines, and children in divorced families are twice as likely to commit or attempt suicide. Larger societal effects on children also include the fact that girls whose fathers leave before they are five are eight times more likely to experience teen pregnancy. Children have lower GPAs when they are from families with divorced or unmarried parents. Children are also less likely to be in poor health when they are in a nuclear family compared to a family with divorced or unmarried parents. Divorce also has negative effects on the parents that echo through society. Divorce also causes lower incomes for people, which adversely affects the economy and society in general. Women who experience divorce face a 27 percent decrease in standard of living. Unmarried women have a higher likelihood to stay in poverty compared to married women. It would seem obvious that divorce and not getting married are terrible things, but the left somehow still pushes this.

To change minds on the impact of family values, it is important to focus on all of the great things that marriage brings to people and society in general. Married couples drink and smoke less and are in better health overall. Married people are more active in their communities, participating in community service and volunteering. Married people have greater wealth overall, where married men earn 22 percent more than single men. Men also live longer when they are married, and the children of married partners are also happier. Being married is in almost every single way better than the inverse for men, women, and children. You can ask people you're talking to, "Do you think more people being divorced or not getting married has had a positive impact on society?" Most people will say no, and at that point, you can go over all the facts and statistics we have discussed. They will most likely agree with you. Then it is important to bring it back to the question of women's choices in America, as it usually goes back to that anyway. Most people then will say regardless of the negative data, women should be pushed to work like men and be in similar positions as men or remain unmarried if they would like to. Although it is of course true that women should be just as free as men to pursue what they want, ask them, "Do you think pushing women to sacrifice marriage and children for a career that on average makes them unhappy is the best thing we should do?" Most people when given the information about how marriage helps not only the adults but also the children will agree that family values should be prioritized in America.

Chapter 7

. . . .

ABORTION

ONE OF THE most convincing videos I have done is when I went to UCLA to talk to students about the issue of abortion. I asked them about when a fetus is considered a life, about how late someone should be able to abort a baby, and about prenatal screenings. Many of the students I talked to, when asked if a mother should be allowed to abort her child at nine months into pregnancy, said yes, and all of them pointed to the fact that it is a "woman's choice" what to do with her body. This is the crux of the abortion argument. The left has manipulated people into believing that abortion is an issue based on women's rights and women's access to healthcare. This couldn't be further from the truth. The issue of abortion is a human life issue first and foremost, not an issue of the evil patriarchy coming down on women to take their rights away. If you can convince the person you're talking to of that fact, then you will successfully change their mind every time on the issue of abortion.

Abortion is legal up until birth at the federal level in America. The left would love to tell you how terrible it is to try to restrict healthcare to women when you talk about abortion. They label abortion as "healthcare" and a "women's rights issue" to try to shame you from talking about it. They tell you that if you're a man, you can't talk about abortion because you don't have a uterus. In reality, men should speak up the most strongly about abortion. It takes two people to conceive a child, half of that equation being the man, so men have every right to speak on this issue just as much as women. Let's start breaking down some of the arguments.

One of the most widely used and egregious arguments from the left is that the baby inside the mother is just a "clump of cells." Whenever I post something on Face-book or Twitter or Instagram about abortion, this is one of the first arguments I hear from the left without fail. When talking to people about abortion, the setup is very important, and it is imperative that you have your facts right to speak the truth to them to change their minds. It is obviously important to do that on every topic, but with abortion in particular you need to be able to explain to them, through your knowledge, the different stages of life to disprove the "clump of cells" argument entirely.

When arguing with pro-choice people on abortion and the "clump of cells" argument, it is helpful to start at the nine-month mark, asking them if it is okay to abort a child up to that point. If someone says it's okay to abort a child at up to nine months of pregnancy, they first of all probably have some deep-rooted issues in their own life but more importantly are at the most extreme, which means you can work down the whole timeline of pregnancy with them to try to change their mind. By nine months of pregnancy, almost every child is at its most developed in the womb and is ready to come out into the world. Let's imagine a scenario. A woman was told by her doctor that her child would be born on July 4. The woman ends up giving birth on July 3 to a fully healthy, adorable child, one day earlier than the original mark. A person who says an abortion at nine months is totally fine is essentially condemning a fully developed child to death. If that woman in this hypothetical situation would have scheduled to have an abortion on July 3, she would be killing a child who is ready to come out of the womb into the world. Is that right? Is that morally ethical? Think about all the children who are born early and still live amazing, wonderful lives. Albert Einstein was born two months ahead of schedule and ended up living an amazing life and becoming one of the greatest minds the world has ever seen. If someone is aborted at nine months, it is not just unethical; it is murder. An abortionist in a third-trimester abortion will usually first kill the baby by injecting it with a substance that will make it have a heart attack, and then the mother gives birth to the stillborn child. Abortion at all levels is murder, as we will work down to prove, but the pure evil involved with aborting a child at nine months, who is able to come out into the world as a fully functional, healthy human, is beyond sick. There is no "clump of cells" argument that can battle that; it is the killing of a child, and there is no other way around it.

Not everyone is so extreme to say that nine-month abortions should be allowed. Many people know that the child within the womb at that point is a child who is almost ready to come out and it would be unethical to have them aborted. Some people will claim five to six months should be the cutoff, but again, these people most likely do not have all the facts about a baby's development. By 25 weeks, or just over five months, a baby is considered viable. By this time, the baby is developing hair, and by six months the baby begins to hiccup and sleeps and wakes in regular cycles. Its brain tissue continues to develop, and with the right medical care, it could survive outside the womb by itself. All of this data for a five-month baby clearly shows that this is no clump of cells, and thus you have to backtrack even further. You can ask them, if six months isn't okay because the child is more developed than you thought, what about three months? They will probably say it's okay to have an abortion at this point, and then you can push back again. An abortion in the second trimester consists of the doctor dismembering and removing the baby from the mother's uterus. By 20 weeks the baby can feel pain, and its nervous system continues to develop. Its organs are visible even earlier, and its limbs and fingernails continue to develop. Once again, this is not some clump of cells, but a human who can feel pain and is continuing to develop.

The final push on the "clump of cells" argument is within the first trimester after fertilization. Is it still a clump of cells then? An abortion in this trimester usually consists of a woman taking pills that end the baby's life. In the first trimester, the baby is developing its limbs and can open and close its fingers. The child's organs begin to form, and its teeth start to come in, and by just three weeks after fertilization the baby's heart begins to beat. Since when did clumps of cells have organs and a heartbeat? The "clump of cells" argument is a fallacy created by the left to make the child seem like it is meaningless and has no value and to take away its humanity. But in reality, even a fetus the first day after being conceived has humanity. We are all made in

God's image, no matter if you are a day old in the womb or 100 years old. What stage of life you're in doesn't define your humanity; your being a child of God does.

If you know Los Angeles, you know Echo Park, and you know it is one of the most liberal, hippie-dippy places in the city. Knowing this, the only logical thing for me to do was to make a video there talking to leftists about abortion. Great idea, right? I decided to ask people to sign a petition to save eagle eggs that haven't hatched yet, but with a twist. After they signed that one, I brought out the other petition I made, a petition to protect unborn humans in the womb. Many people, when they realized what just happened, were rather upset with me. One girl flipped off the camera, cursed at me, and then walked away. I bring this up to show the emotion that people attach to this issue. When their notions are challenged on abortion, especially women, it is very easy for people to get upset because the left has made this issue indispensable to women's rights. But when you can convince people of the value of life and that life starts at conception, you can take away a lot of the negative emotions they may have. But it definitely isn't always easy.

When I first started becoming a conservative and a Christian, abortion was *the* issue my liberal friends could not get on board with. Speaking up for the unborn was the number one topic I would get shamed on almost every day on campus. I would go to the main quad with pro-life signs and a table and debate people for hours on the issue, and almost every single time there was some lefty woman or liberal dude in a camo jacket yelling at me and berating me for my pro-life stance. They screamed at me and called me sexist and fascist for wanting to preserve a human life. The point these people were missing is that they had been fooled to believe that a child in the womb is a part of the woman's body and not a distinct human. As soon as sperm meets egg, life begins. Life 100 percent begins at conception, but the left fails to recognize this fact despite always claiming they are the "party of science." They should try reading the countless medical textbooks or talking to the hundreds of doctors who would all agree on this fact.

The key thing that really woke me up to the evils of abortion is when I realized the sanctity of human life. Life is full of infinite opportunities, whereas death is so final, and every child that is aborted loses all potential to have an amazing, passion-filled life. Justin Bieber's mother was encouraged to abort her child and almost did it but instead she chose to keep it and gave birth to baby Justin. There are countless cases of women who have thought about abortion and almost gone through with it but decided against it and gave birth to the child instead, saving that child's life. Many people when told this will say how "unfair it is to be born into a terrible situation or a terrible life." This is a ludicrous argument. Except in maybe some of the most extreme and abhorrent circumstances, there is no possible scenario where the possibility of life is worse than never being born. Again, life has infinite opportunities, whereas death has none. Millions of people every year are born into terrible circumstances and turn their lives into wonderful and amazing success stories. This is the beauty of life, that anyone despite their circumstances can have the ability to make something incredible out of their existence. With abortion being so prevalent, think about all of the millions of lives that were halted and the millions of potential doctors, scientists, and amazing people who could have been born. It is truly a horrific thing to think about and, when pressed on pro-choice people, should hopefully make them just as sad with you.

"MY BODY, MY CHOICE!!!" This is another one of the main talking points the harpies would scream at me on campus. For such a common argument, it couldn't be further from the truth. How the left can conflate a living child growing and living inside a woman as part of her body is completely beyond me. A pimple on your face is a part of your body. It is connected to you and is not a new, living organism. A child inside a woman has a completely different set of DNA and genetics than the mother and is only a "part of her body" in the sense that it is living inside her. But if a tapeworm came and lived in your stomach, would you consider that a part of your body? Of course not. Living inside the mother does not constitute a part of her body, only that the mother provides the nutrients needed for the baby to survive. Is the fact that the mother has to provide nutrients to the child and care for it justification for abortion? Well, a mother will provide all the care and nutrition for a baby even when it is out of the womb, so that counter-point from the left doesn't work either. What about the fact that a child in the womb would die if it wasn't for the mother providing for it? Well, could a one-year-old baby survive without its mother outside the womb? Of course not, so that argument is also null. Every single pro-choice argument can be broken down with proper logic and reasoning, which is why the main arguments from the left turn the conversation away from abortion as a human life issue to a women's rights issue.

But what about the rights of the baby? We have already established that it is a life from conception and that the mother has a responsibility to take care of it, so shouldn't the living child inside the mother have rights as well? This is how the debate should end. When I talked to people at the UCLA campus about abortion, I ended with this question, and most of the people I talked to had one simple last point that you have probably heard before. "I would never get an abortion myself, but if someone else wants to, I think it's okay." This is how you know you have won the debate, and I feel bad for people who make this argument. They have been so shamed by the left to support abortion that even when their own minds are changed, they still continue to say they support it for other people. At this point you finish and ask, "If it is immoral and murder for you, why would it not be for someone else?" And then the debate is done. Don't be discouraged if this is how they end the debate; you can be happy that you at least changed *their* mind. That's a lot more than Republicans have done on this issue over the past 60 years.

When you speak up for the unborn, the left will cast you off as old news. They say you don't care about women, you're a religious extremist, or you're living in the past. But none of that is true. Sixty-one million babies have been killed by abortion since *Roe v. Wade*, and by any measure of the word, this is genocide. When you stand up to put an end to abortion, you *are* showing you care about women, mothers, and all the unborn women across the country. It is a lonely road to go down to stand up for the unborn, but it is the only morally right road to go down, and moving forward, you should walk it proudly.

Chapter 8

· · · · · · · · · · ·

POLICE BRUTALITY

KEITH KONOPASEK was the type of guy everyone liked to be around. He was friendly and funny and had a stellar mustache. He's the type of guy you could just sit down and have a beer with and have a great time. He lived in northern California in the 1990s and decided to become a police officer. He first tried to get a job in the San Jose police department, but they told him they already had too many white police officers due to their affirmative action standards, so he decided to become a cop in the much less safe Oakland community nearby, where they always needed new officers to work the dangerous, crime-ridden neighborhoods. He graduated from the academy at the top of his class in January 1995, worked with a training officer until April of the same year, and after that he was out in his own patrol car by himself.

It was a warm July night in Oakland, and Officer Keith was working the beat in a bad part of town when he saw a drug deal take place on a corner that was well known for crime. He turned on his lights and sirens and followed the car of one of the guys he just saw involved with the drug deal. Officer Keith pulled the man over in a nearby neighborhood, and another police officer arrived on the scene shortly after. After a quick back-and-forth, the man in question was put in the back of the second police car, and the two officers began to search the vehicle. The first officer searched the driver's side, so Keith searched the passenger side. It was looking to be a routine search with nothing too out of the ordinary until something happened that no one expected. As Keith was bent over searching the car, the man who lived in the house right in front of the street they were on looked through his screen door, took aim with his illegal assault weapon, and shot Officer Keith from behind. Because he was bent over, the bullet went through him from below and ended up coming out the top of his shoulder, completely destroying him internally. The man who shot Officer Keith was a black man named Clarence Thomas Jones who had just been laid off by the security company he worked for. The Oakland police had been investigating his company for allegedly doing shady security, and so to cover its tracks, it was laying off employees, and Clarence happened to be one of them. Clarence was an excellent shot, and the bullet hit the target exactly how he planned.

Officer Keith didn't survive the shooting, and his family and the community were devastated. What's even worse is that Clarence, the man who shot Keith, was let off with nothing due to the jury. The district attorney later told the defense that if Keith had been black and the shooter had been white, their case would have had a chance in civil court, but alas, Clarence walked off scot-free and moved to North Carolina with nothing on his record even showing that he had killed a police officer. Keith was only 32 when he died, and in a terrible chance of fate, on July 8, the same day he was shot and killed, his wedding invitation arrived in the mail.

This is the tragic and heartbreaking story of Officer Keith Konopasek, the uncle of an old friend of mine. Their family was ravaged by this, and sadly, this story is not uncommon. Police officers put their lives on the line to keep our communities safe every day, leaving their house not knowing if they are going to come back. The left will tell you how terrible the police are and how racist and violent they act while referring to them as an entity instead of actual people, but they refuse to look at the actual data. A police officer is 18.5 times more likely to be killed by a black man in the line of duty than a black man is to be killed by police. Heroes like Keith work tirelessly every day to keep Americans safe but get treated like absolute filth by the mainstream media and far-left activists. Police officers don't do it for the money, they don't do it for power, and they definitely don't do it for fame. They put up with the slander and danger because they care about America and want to protect it. The left drags police officers through the mud while ignoring the data and denying them their humanity, treating them more like literal pigs than actual people. Every officer has a story, and the left, the so-called "party of love and tolerance," should shift their focus away from their demonization of good, hardworking officers and shift it toward recognizing the incredible heroism we see done by these brave men and women of the law every single day.

If you ask most liberals in America what the biggest issue facing black Americans is, they would all most likely say racism and police brutality. After the death of George Floyd in May 2020 by a white police officer, thousands upon thousands of people took to the streets and protested, demanding justice and police reform. Many of the protests turned violent, and after those first protests, we have seen a dramatic increase in the amount of rioting and looting in America. It seems like now anytime a black man is killed by police, the left uses it as a justification to destroy their own cities, no matter whether the police officer was justified in their actions. Throughout 2020, ACAB, which stands for All Cops Are Bastards, has become one of the most popular terms used by the left to describe our police when they riot. We've heard chants to defund the police, chants to disband the police, and even chants to kill the police. The saddest part about all of this is that the people protesting the cops and asking for them to be killed are the same people that the police work tirelessly every single day to defend. It would be funny if it weren't so depressing.

I've made a few videos on the street asking people about the police and have talked to experts and police officers about what's going on in America as well. In one of my favorite videos, I went out to Venice Beach in California and asked people about the number of people the police kill every year, specifically black people. When I asked a group of young black men what they thought about the police, one of them said that the police are "out looking for another neck to put their knee on. That's how they really feel." That is the mindset of millions of Americans right now about the cops. I then pressed them further, as I was hoping to change their minds. I asked them how many unarmed black men were killed by police in 2019. One said 500; another said 1,500. Again, this is what millions of Americans think about the cops, and it's incredibly sad to see the vilification of so many good police officers. What are the actual numbers? you might be asking. Well, let's break down some of the data on police officers in this country and give you the ammunition you need to defend cops every time someone brings them up.

The first question is, are the police racist? The short answer is no, and the data absolutely backs that up. More white people are killed by police every year than black people. All deaths in any situation are a tragedy, but the data just doesn't show that the police have a pattern of racism. In 2017, 457 white people were shot to death by police, where only 223 black people were killed by police. That is more than double the number of white people to black people. In 2018 and 2019, the numbers were similar. Now, people might say that's because there are just more white people in this country than black people; it doesn't mean the police aren't racist. Well, then let's look at crime proportionally. Despite making up 24 percent of the population in Houston, black people commit 58 percent of crimes that usually lead to death from a police officer. These include aggravated assault on a peace officer, attempted capital murder on a peace officer, evading arrest, resisting arrest, and interfering in an arrest. So even despite black people committing a higher volume of these types of crimes than white people, white people are still fatally shot by police officers more times every year than black people. In Houston, the police say that over half of the dangerous situations they encounter involve black people. This isn't racist; this is the truth.

But what about all the unarmed people killed by police officers? What about those 1,500 unarmed blacks that man I talked to said had been killed by police? In reality, the number is much smaller than that. In 2019, only 14 unarmed black men were fatally shot by police. Far off from the number in the hundreds that many people would guess it is. In California, only one unarmed black man was killed by police in 2019, in contrast to the four unarmed white men killed by police in California in the same year. In the whole country in 2019, an additional 24 unarmed white men were fatally shot by police. We can first gather that there is no epidemic of unarmed black people being fatally shot by police— 14 is an incredibly low number—but we can also once again see that the data does not show an anomaly for black people. Once again, more unarmed white people are killed by police than black people, disproving the lies of the left claiming police officers target black people. According to the Manhattan Institute, there are

7,500 black homicide victims every year. Only 0.2 percent of that would include those 14 unarmed black men shot by police. That number is negligible in comparison to the vast number of other black murder victims every year, most of whom are killed by other blacks.

Millions of people in America aren't looking at the data and continue to scream for the defunding of the police. In some cities across the country, those cries for defunding have been heard and answered and have been met with terrible consequences. I still remember being in high school in 2014 and hearing about Michael Brown being shot fatally by police in Ferguson, Missouri. At this point I was still in my liberal phase of life, and I believed this was a completely racist act. An unarmed black man was just walking down the street, and a white police officer decided to shoot him. That was the narrative we got, and it is still the narrative millions of people believe today, but it couldn't be further from the truth. The truth is that Michael Brown was stopped by police because he matched the description of someone who had just robbed a convenience store. He punched an officer through an opening in a window, tried to steal the cop's gun, and then ran. He never said the famous line "Hands up don't shoot!" and was charging toward Officer Darren Wilson when he got shot, not running away. Finally, a local grand jury and a federal investigation both found Officer Wilson was fair in his use of force. But none of this matters. What matters is that a white officer killed an unarmed black man, and the mainstream media, Hollywood, and the radical left twisted it into a racist narrative that ended up helping start the Black Lives Matter movement.

To the left, the facts of these incidents don't matter. After Michael Brown's story hit the media, Ferguson erupted with rioting, looting, and violence. Many people protested peacefully, but hundreds of others took to the streets, vandalizing and destroying buildings, hurting people, and causing millions of dollars' worth of damage. After the riots settled down, Ferguson, and the rest of America, took a long, hard look at its policing and vowed to invest in antiracist policing practices. As police officers saw the lack of support they were getting from heads of departments and how Officer Wilson had been dragged through the mud after he shot Michael Brown, many cops were incredibly scared to do their job. Michael Brown was fatally shot in 2014, and in 2015 and 2016 there were an additional 2,000 black homicide victims, in comparison to 2014. This is what Heather Mac Donald called the Ferguson Effect. As police are disrespected, lied about, and eventually defunded, crime will increase. As we take away police officers' resources and funding and make them feel like they are all racist, we don't see less crime, we see more of it.

After the death of George Floyd by white cop Derek Chauvin in the spring of 2020, we saw the Ferguson Effect in full swing once again. Derek Chauvin murdered George Floyd and was rightly punished for it, but the demonization of cops across the country after this one incident spread like wildfire, and riots and crime broke out in many major U.S. cities. New York City cut the police force by 2,500 members and has seen a 127 percent increase in shootings in the city. Six hundred plainclothes officers in an anti-crime unit were reassigned in 2020, and that same week there were 38 shooting victims. That is in comparison to 12 for the same week the year before. Instead of investing in more policing or hiring new officers, Bill de Blasio, mayor of New York City, decided it would be better to invest that money in more social causes. The social justice left has taken over the political arena, and their Defund the Police message is actively killing people. Even Democratic NYC councilman Robert Holden said, "We can't legislate using fashionable slogans that fit on protest signs. It hurts every New Yorker. The NYPD are the gold standard for law enforcement around the world. Any issues that need to be addressed require more training, which costs money." The radical left is pushing Defund the Police, which in turn initiates the Ferguson Effect, which is now destroying American cities and lives in the process. Milwaukee has seen a 132 percent increase in homicides. Baltimore has more murders than ever recorded in that city. The left's anti-police agenda isn't about racism or helping people; it is about virtue signaling and making it seem like you're actually doing something righteous when in reality you are hurting the very people you were hoping to garner support from.

Police risk their lives every day to defend *you*. Of course, there are bad cops, and they should be held accountable for their actions, but the vast majority of police officers are great men and women who defend this country bravely. When the left pushes for defunding the police, treats cops like garbage, and calls for them to be killed, why would anyone want to be a police officer? You first of all take money away from the force, which disincentivizes new people to join and makes it so people already within won't want to stay. It then makes it so that the only people who will join will be bottom-of-the-barrel people with no other options. If you thought you had poorly trained officers now—just wait for the next classes of officers to graduate who are dragged through the dirt by the media and make a fraction of what they once would have made. Nobody wants to go through that, and by treating the cops so poorly, you are destroying the future integrity of all police officers, the opposite effect of what you had planned.

When I went out with Brandon Tatum, a retired police officer, on Hollywood Boulevard to ask people questions about the police, we were able to change the mind of every single person we talked to. Even better, many of the people who we talked to were so happy we stopped them to talk, one girl even thanking us so much for the information that she had never heard before. I think most people, when presented with the facts about police officers, can be very receptive to them, especially when so many people have interacted with the police before or have personal memories with them. The rapper Lil Wayne was pressured on TV to talk about Black Lives Matter and hate on the police, but he wouldn't do it. When he was a little boy, a police officer helped him out of a bad situation, and he was thankful for the police, not resentful toward them. With this issue it's all about stating the facts through questions and then turning back to personal questions. It's easy to start out with the question "How many unarmed black men did police officers kill in 2019?" and get their response. After educating them on the real numbers with that response, they will most likely be shocked, and then you can press on. You then can ask them, "What's more likely, a police officer killing a black man in the line of duty or a black man killing a police officer?" and then once again educate them and move to the end of the conversation. It is good to qualify something similar to this at the end: "Of course we should want the best-trained police in the world, and any bad police officers should be dealt with, but when you defund the police, you only open communities up to more crime, and you make the problem worse. We can't seriously disband the police, and what if someone came to attack you or your loved ones? Who would you call if not the police?" They will have to agree with you at that point, and you should have successfully changed another mind on the issue of police brutality. The vast majority of police officers out there are awesome people, working hard to keep you and our communities safe. If you can convince them of that fact, then any mind can be woken up to the dangers of defunding and disbanding the boys in blue.

Chapter 9

....

CULTURAL
APPROPRIATION

I T WAS OCTOBER 2018, and I was still in my first year as an "influencer" at PragerU. As it got closer to Halloween, cultural appropriation was in the news and all over social media, with warnings reminding people to not be offensive this holiday season. "MY CULTURE IS NOT YOUR DAMN COSTUME" was plastered all over every lefty's Facebook page, and people who were deemed offensive were given monikers like "culture vulture" and "racist." Being the sometimes-mischievous guy I was, who was willing to go to the extreme to prove a point, I decided to make a video on the topic of cultural appropriation. I thought about it with my team at PragerU, and we eventually decided on the idea that I should dress up in traditional Mexican garb and see what students at the University of California, Los Angeles thought about it, but with a twist. See, I wasn't

137

just going out there to terrorize the students and get a sensational video of them calling me racist and the like; I was there to prove a point, and, oh man, did I ever.

The video didn't actually start at UCLA; it started on Olvera Street, a heavily Hispanic area in Los Angeles where street vendors sell all sorts of traditional Mexican food and cultural items. I bought a Mexican poncho and a sombrero and with my fake taped-on mustache went around to all the Mexicans in the area asking them their opinions on my costume. At first, I felt a little silly, but in no time, with my Mexican cameraman by my side, any doubts I had about this video were cast aside. I talked to a lot of Mexicans that day on Olvera Street, and not one of them was offended by my costume. In fact, they all loved it! One of them even called me "muy guapo!" despite figuring out that my mustache was not real. None of the Mexicans I talked to thought it was offensive, and they were happy I was celebrating their culture. Many of the Mexicans I talked to were actually from Mexico as well, not children of people from Mexico. They were the real deal, and they loved what I was wearing and were all about it. If only I could say the same for the students at UCLA...

When I pulled up to the UCLA campus in my outfit, as soon as I walked out of my car, I started getting rough looks. My cameraman Rodrigo and I looked at each other, and we both shared the same expression. "Here we go!" I exclaimed as I walked into the quad ready for the onslaught of what was about to happen. Within five seconds of getting to the main intersection of the campus, I was getting insults hurled at me. "Go home, racist!" and "Cultural appropriation!" were some of the milder ones sent my way, but not everyone was so gentle with the things they yelled at me. Many people cursed at me and said horrible things as they walked by, and I'm not gonna lie, I felt pretty awkward. But I laughed it off, reapplied my fake mustache, and started questioning the students. The results were what you would imagine. All the privileged white students said I was racist; they said the costume was cultural appropriation and that I shouldn't be wearing something that wasn't my culture. It's funny—many of them called *me* privileged for wearing that costume around campus, and what's even funnier is that many said if Mexicans saw that they would be incredibly offended. Ha! If only they knew where I just came from!

Eventually I told them who sold me the costume, and their minds started to open ever so slightly, but they still thought I was racist. But once I told them how the Mexicans loved my costume, literally showing them pictures of me with the Mexicans from Olvera Street on my phone celebrating and laughing, they were now the embarrassed ones. A bunch of white people coming and telling me I'm racist for celebrating another culture, a culture that isn't even theirs to defend in the first place. These students were white knighting and virtue signaling for the Mexicans without realizing that their actions and thoughts about me were *actually* the real racism in this situation. It is racist to think that Mexican people are too shy and weak to defend themselves from white people wearing sombreros and that you as a white person have to defend them. If Mexican people really wanted white people to stop dressing up in their garb, they would say something themselves, not wait around shyly for white college students to do it. The college students used the Mexican people as a prop for their social justice causes and virtue signaling, and in turn, all parties were hurt in that situation. I explained this to many students and changed the minds not only of them but also of the tens of millions of people who have watched that video. To this day, it is still one of my favorite videos I have ever done, and when fans come up to me on the street or out and about, this is almost always one of the videos they list as a favorite of mine.

This video isn't people's favorite video just because it's funny and entertaining, even though it is. It is people's favorite video because it is irrefutable evidence that the left is wrong about the issue of cultural appropriation. It proves a definitive point: that the people who are supposed to be offended by these things aren't offended at all. Is that one video not enough proof for you? Well, for Halloween the next year, I did the same thing, this time dressing up in traditional Chinese attire, starting in Chinatown and asking Chinese people what they thought and then going back to UCLA. Once again, the Chinese people loved it, and the leftist students hated it. Some students even recognized me as the Mexican guy from the year before, and they came back around to call me racist once again. But once they talked to me, I changed even more minds when I showed them the truth of the issue. The left is wrong about cultural appropriation. There are no ifs, ands, or buts. They are *wrong*.

Would it surprise you to hear that the issue of cultural appropriation was first talked about by white people? "Cultural colonialism" was first coined by the white man Kenneth Couts-Smith when he brought in Marxist ideas to talk about "class appropriation." Then in 1994, white guy Michael North, in his book *The Dialect of Modernism*, discussed "voice appropriation." All of these concepts have come together to make the term "cultural appropriation," which is so prevalent throughout the American lexicon today. When you're talking to people about cultural appropriation, it's important to talk to them about who the appropriation is actually negatively affecting. When I have made all my videos about the topic, it is always white people or people who don't belong to the culture I am allegedly "appropriating" who are the angriest with me. This is not a coincidence. Many white leftists take on the battle of cultural appropriation as, pun not intended, white knights, trying to "save" the minorities who can't defend themselves from the evil white man dressing up as someone of their culture. But this is all a farce. Minorities aren't asking you to get offended for them; you're doing it for yourself and so that other people around you will think you're "woke." But let me tell you something, white leftists. There is nothing "woke" about caring about the feelings and emotions of these minorities when you then turn around and advocate for the same leftist programs and policies that have kept minorities down in America for decades.

Let's look at a real-world example of the dismantling of cultural appropriation that isn't just one of my videos. In 2015, the Boston Museum of Fine Arts hosted an exhibit that was meant to showcase the beauty of traditional Japanese clothing by having people show up wearing kimonos and celebrating Japanese culture. After this event went viral on social media, protestors showed up to the museum, mostly white women, claiming the museum was racist and appropriating Japanese culture. Signs were held up that said, "Not your Asian fetish" and "Decolonize our museums," and the museum put out an apology. But despite all this backlash, what did the Japanese community in Boston think of the exhibit? Well, many Japanese people actually counterprotested the mostly white crowd of protestors protesting the museum. Many Japanese women wanted the museum to return to its original "Kimono Wednesdays" programming, and Etsuko Yashiro, a Japanese woman who helped organize the Boston Japan festival, said that she was trying to share the beauty of kimonos with an American audience. Another counterprotester, Ikuko Burns, a woman born in Tokyo who then moved to America, said she used to take traditional Japanese kimonos to schools as a consultant for the children's museum to teach children about traditional Japanese culture. Once again, this is another "cultural appropriation" story where people who aren't part of the affected group get offended on behalf of the group that is supposed to be offended. The counterprotesters weren't a bunch of white conservatives coming to own the libs or talk about the politically correct culture of the left; they were Japanese Americans, coming to prove the point that they were *not* offended and were happy that the Boston Museum of Fine Arts had put their culture on display for all to see. They were happy for the exhibit and were not ashamed by another culture sharing their ideas and traditions but enthralled by it, reveling in the idea that Americans wanted to share their culture.

Let's look at a study, one even done by the very left-leaning *Washington Post*, which found that 9 out of 10 Native Americans weren't offended by the Washington Redskins football team name. Leftists will pressure you and tell you how terrible that name is and how racist it is to Native Americans, but at least 90 percent of Native Americans themselves aren't at all offended by the name. Many of them actually like the name, as it shows Native Americans in a positive light, showcasing them as strong warriors who won't be defeated in battle or, in this case, on the football field. This should hold true to all of us. If I heard there was going to be a new football team named for average height, skinny white guys, I would be thrilled! It is a celebration of different cultures, not an exercise in racism or cultural appropriation. Native Americans like the name Redskins because it exudes strength, not weakness, and the fact that the National Football League named a team after them is a sign of respect, not racism.

Wouldn't you want people of other cultures celebrating your successes or joining together in your culture? What is racist about wanting to enjoy someone else's amazing culture yourself? Sure, there are times when you can be degrading another culture, such as making a caricature of another culture or being malicious in your depiction, but for the most part, most people engaging in the left's definition of "cultural appropriation" are merely trying to celebrate or, at the very least, take part in another person's culture. America is the magical and amazing place it is because of the amalgamation of cultures we have present within it. Whether that's going to a sushi place on your favorite street in town, buying traditional Native American jewelry, or celebrating St. Patrick's Day with everyone else, America is a wonderful place because all of these different cultures can coexist as one. There is nowhere else in the world where this mix of different languages and cultures is as evident as in America, and we are the greatest country in the world because of it. But the left wants to take this appreciation of cultures and turn it into shame, taking what would have been seen as celebrating another culture's identity and heritage and now seeing it as hating it or "appropriating" it. It is a twisted message that only aims to further divide this country and allow leftists another chance to virtue signal while accomplishing nothing.

It is important to always expose the hypocrisy of the left to the people on the left who you talk to. Blue jeans were invented in America and are a huge part of our culture. Is it cultural appropriation if another culture wears those? What about if people in Mexico celebrate the Fourth of July because they appreciate this country? Should they be "canceled" for that? The answer is, of course not, but it leaves leftists stumped when pressed with the question of other people appropriating American culture. If you can convince people of the hypocrisy of their own arguments while also showing them real-world examples of the truth, you can easily change their minds on the issue of cultural appropriation.

Chapter 10

. . . .

CANCEL CULTURE

THE CONCEPT OF cancel culture is a relatively new phenomenon that was born out of the rise of social media but has really become prevalent in the last few years as leftists have gotten more and more dogmatic. The act of "canceling" someone is when you get massive support for the destruction of someone's career, reputation, or livelihood, typically by calling them out on something they did or said. What is so bad about that? People doing and saying bad things getting called out for their behavior seems like it should be an admirable thing, right? The problem doesn't lie in calling people out for disgusting actions; it lies in destroying people for things and sending an angry mob toward them when they voice a different opinion.

J. K. Rowling is the world-famous author of the *Harry Potter* series of children's books. I personally think *The*

Lord of the Rings is 1,000 times better as a series, but that's neither here nor there. Regardless, J. K. Rowling for years has been heralded as an icon for strong liberal women, putting themes of social justice within her novels and being proud of doing so. In 2016, right before the presidential election, J. K. Rowling put out a tweet calling Donald Trump "a giant orange twitter egg," along with other tweets about how she did not support him or his campaign. She would be considered a liberal, by all definitions of the word, if not a leftist, and was celebrated as a champion of women's rights. But in 2019, everything changed when J. K. Rowling was deemed canceled by the left for a tweet she made defending a woman who got fired. Rowling tweeted, "Dress however you please. Call yourself whatever you like. Sleep with any consenting adult who'll have you, Live your best life in peace and security. But force women out of their jobs for stating that sex is real?" She wrote this after it went public that a woman got fired for making remarks stating that women lose out on safety when transgender women with male genitals are in the same locker room as them and that transgender women are not women. After J. K. Rowling tweeted this, the LGBT community on Twitter went after her for it, and they canceled her. One Twitter user said, "Hi. breaking my hiatus real quick just to say: f--- what your childhood heroes say. trans people are real." This tweet, along with thousands of others, condemned Rowling for her words, but they didn't just stop at condemnation; they meant to destroy her.

J. K. Rowling's situation is not an uncommon occurrence. People on social media get canceled every day for miscellaneous comments and actions that showcase a difference of opinion or are just benign in general. Twitter is littered on the daily with trending hashtag #thispersonisoverparty, and the Explore page is covered with "breaking news" of the latest person to say something outside the left wing's doctrine. The cancel police don't just go after conservatives either. Like with J. K. Rowling, you can be a leftist and still get canceled. The left takes no prisoners, and if you don't agree with their agenda 100 percent, you will be destroyed. Even the smallest stray away from left-wing dogma and you will be canceled.

I remember when they tried to "cancel" me for the first time. It was 2019, and the year before I had made a video where I ranted about the problem with multiculturalism in Europe. In 2018 when I posted it, not too many people saw the video, and nothing really happened. It was a good video, full of facts and research to back up my claims, and after I made it, I didn't expect a whole lot of pushback. A year later, PragerU posted the video again as it became relevant, and on Twitter, all hell broke loose. Some blue-checkmark leftists first saw the video on the PragerU page, and after a few of them retweeted with some snarky comments, thousands upon thousands of people started flooding all of my social media pages commenting on the video, sending me death threats, calling me a "racist" and a "Nazi," and telling me I should be canceled. There was an entire mob, thousands strong, trying to get me deplatformed and my career ruined and destroyed. To those of you who have never been "canceled" before, it's definitely a strange thing to have happen to you. Imagine hundreds of people you've never met vying for a chance to virtue signal and earn their 15 seconds of social media fame commenting on your posts and wishing nothing more than to have your entire livelihood be taken away from you, just because you don't agree with their politics. The moral of the story is, the world is a cruel place, and people can be absolutely terrible. Social media brings out the worst in people, and when people get together behind seeing someone ruined, they can be vicious and unrelenting. It's very easy online away from real people to anonymously say horrible things when thousands of others are doing the same, and thus cancel culture is born. Cancel culture is a product of people without anything valuable or interesting to bring to the table themselves, so all they do is herd together like sheep, shaming people who actually stand up for something different to make themselves feel "special." Cancel culture is a cancer and has to be stopped.

Many people get canceled for things that are deemed offensive that they might have said years ago. Once it is uncovered that they said something offensive or wrong, the mob comes after them. Frankly, I could care less what someone said 10 years ago. If a politician or celebrity or influencer said something gross, dumb, or nasty in their past but is now a changed, more mature person and no longer represents what they said, I see no reason to cancel them. Again, people who want to cancel someone for something they said 10 years ago need a reality check, and I can guarantee you that if their life and everything they had ever said was under the microscope, the cancel mob could come after them as well. It's easy to point your finger at someone else when you're behind a screen or people aren't looking at your life; it's hard to stand up for someone being attacked. You have to use your best judgment when it comes to each individual situation, but I always err on the side of defending whoever is getting attacked. When I see leftists on Twitter getting attacked for a "bigoted" remark they made years and years ago, I don't rush to call them out for it. As soon as you do that, you are part of the mob. The best thing to do in these situations is not to "cancel" them over their past behavior but to look at the things they are *currently* doing and call them out for those actions. People shouldn't have their lives destroyed over stupid things they said years ago if they have changed for the better, and as a conservative who doesn't believe in cancel culture, you can't pick and choose based on politics for whom you "cancel." That is what the left does. People should be held account-able for their actions and things they say, but look at who they are currently, not who some journalist with an agenda on Twitter claims them to be. Whether they are on the left or the right, it doesn't matter; you should defend people who are attacked by the mob.

Of course, there are egregious situations where peo-ple should be canceled. Harvey Weinstein, Kevin Spacey, and people who are accused of committing real crimes should be lambasted and made an example of when the evidence is clear that they did something vile and wrong. But people who have a different opinion from you, or someone who made some little mistake years ago and is now getting killed on social media, should not be "canceled." When talking to people about cancel culture, it's important to make this distinction. Certain people should be canceled, but destroying someone's livelihood over a difference in politics is a malady. Earlier in 2020, Chris Pratt got canceled after people on Twitter saw he went to church and didn't attend a Joe Biden campaign rally with the rest of the cast from *The Avengers*. They claimed he had homophobic, white supremacist energy and that he should be canceled. So even when the left has no evidence, they are fine with canceling someone if they just feel like it or they go against the grain. When talking to people about cancel culture, there are a few key questions to ask. First ask them, "If you say something that demonstrates a difference of opinion from someone else, should you be attacked?" Many will answer yes, and then you can follow up by asking them, "Should someone who has a difference of opinion have their career destroyed for it?" This will put them in a situation where they will answer differently if you're talking to them in person. For the most part, if you ask someone this question in person, you can tell by their expression and body language that they will feel bad. They don't want to destroy people's lives, but when they're online with no repercussions, they are fine with doing it. It is imperative to press them on the destruction of people's lives, careers, and reputations and put them in that person's shoes. You will change their mind if you can make them empathize with the people who are being "canceled" and make them understand what it would be like for them if they were to be attacked by the social media mob. Again, put them in the other person's shoes; ask them if they have ever said anything before in their entire lives that would threaten to have them canceled. Everyone should say yes, even begrudgingly so, and you can then press them on whether they think their career or reputation should be ruined because of that one thing they said before in their lives that may not have been the greatest. I believe cancel culture is a relatively easy issue to change people's minds on, and I think the culture online is already starting to shift away from canceling anyone who has done or said something "off." If the left tries to cancel everybody for every menial thing, then the act of canceling means nothing, and the real criminals and disgusting people out there who truly deserve to be canceled won't see the proper justice from the public eye.

Chapter 11

· · · · · · · · · · ·

CLIMATE CHANGE

T WAS 2019, and I was interviewing people at a march put on by Extinction Rebellion, a group aimed at stopping the end of the world due to climate change. Before arriving, I had the brilliant idea of growing out a mustache (which is always a brilliant idea for all you men reading this), disguising myself as a leftist, and creating a petition. The paper on the clipboard had a fake vow I was asking for signatures for, a vow that asked people to stop having children due to climate change. You wouldn't believe the number of signatures I got. Young and old leftists from all races lined up to sign and dedicate their lives to stopping the world from ending due to nasty children coming and polluting and destroying the earth. It truly was a sight to behold. I asked one man to sign, and he said he was already doing his part. He had gotten a vasectomy for climate change. The level of

delusion at this march was unreal. Eventually I was dis-
covered, my disguise was busted, and we were forced to
leave, but not before we made the point with this video:
that the climate movement was not about actually protecting the world or being environmentally conscious
but about fear and an anti-human agenda.

When I was in elementary school, I couldn't tell you
what a Republican or Democrat was, I couldn't tell you
about the three branches of government, and I couldn't
explain the electoral college. But I could tell you that
global warming was a huge issue and the world was
dying. The propaganda started that early, and despite
having no real research to back up my claims about
global warming at that young age, I just knew it was
true. The climate change movement is insidious and
intertwined with our public school system to get kids
hooked on the global warming hysteria early, which
makes this a very difficult topic to speak to people about
and change their minds on. This is one issue where
the facts really are more important than just asking
questions in a persuasive way because the indoctrination runs so deep and people need tangible evidence
to change their mind. I still remember being in elementary school when climate change was referred to
as global warming, but the left changed the name to
the more easily provable climate change when global

warming was debunked. The climate is always changing, but the globe might not necessarily be warming due to human actions, so they changed the name to keep the hysteria alive without sacrificing any of the control. The climate change movement is incredibly manipulative and works through fear of the apocalypse to control people and bend them to support it. But with the right facts and strategy you can change everyone's mind on this issue.

The claim that we have twelve years left to save the planet has been thrown around by many prominent leftists like Alexandria Ocasio-Cortez, and when I talk to leftists on campuses and on the streets, they echo the same declaration. But is the world really ending? Do we really have 12 years left? The answer is obviously no, but let's look at some of the reasons why. The Intergovernmental Panel on Climate Change, or IPCC for short, showed no evidence in its report on climate change that the world was going to end in 12 years or that billions of people were going to die. It didn't claim that mass migration was happening because of climate change or that people would be displaced because of climate change, but it did claim that economic and social reasons were a much bigger factor in all those things. The IPCC also had "low confidence" that there were going to be more natural disasters because of climate change.

Yes, there's more damage from natural disasters now than ever before, a fact leftists use to cite that natural disasters are getting worse, but this is only because there are more buildings and infrastructure around now as humans have economically advanced. With more buildings, that means that natural disasters have more structures to damage. They aren't getting worse or killing more people, just causing more damage because of humans' increased wealth.

Al Gore is one of the biggest climate change apocalypse professors around, and he has made some absolutely outrageous predictions. His 2006 documentary *An Inconvenient Truth* was a massive success and was seen millions of times, and it was full of doomsday claims and fearmongering. It also made him millions of dollars and into an even bigger celebrity. But Al Gore would never just make this movie for the clout, right? He definitely fact-checked everything he said in the movie and all of his claims have come true, right? Let's look at some of these claims, shall we?

One claim he made, which when I was a boy made me very sad, was that polar bears were going to drown. If you're anything like me, hearing that polar bears are all going to die is devastating news. The claim was that their habitats were being destroyed because as the earth heated up, their habitats melted, and they were going to be extinct. For anyone who loves cute little polar bear cubs, hearing this news would definitely make you want to do something about climate change. But the truth is that polar bears haven't gone extinct since those claims were made. In fact, there are more polar bears now than there were at the time the claim was made, with an estimated 30,000 polar bears living today in the wild. Another claim made by Mr. Gore was "Within a decade, there will be no more snows on Kilimanjaro." But despite his predictions, Mount Kilimanjaro still has snow in 2021. Even in 2018, 12 years after his prediction, Mount Kilimanjaro had one of the biggest snowfalls on its glaciers that it has had in years. In my opinion, these are just two of the myriad false claims made by Al Gore. And as you might expect, he doesn't even believe in his own claims.

If Al Gore believes that sea levels are rising and climate change is such a massive issue, then why is he buying oceanfront property in Montecito, California? Why are numerous celebrities and politicians who talk about climate change also buying beachfront property and flying on carbon-emitting private jets? Why do the people to whom so many look to give them information about climate change continually lie to us and go against their own teachings? It is because they don't actually believe what they say. Al Gore made $70 million selling his company Current TV to Qatar, one of the most oil-rich countries in the world. If he really believed fossil fuels were destroying the planet, why would he even associate with Qatar? When you dive a little deeper and start looking at not just what the climate hysteria advocates say but what they actually *do,* it's clear they don't actually practice what they preach and are using the gullible people across the world who see a polar bear slipping off a piece of ice to fund their lavish lifestyles and make them incredibly famous. Al Gore, Barack Obama, Leonardo DiCaprio, and all the others who preach the end times don't really believe what they're saying, but they've convinced millions of people across the globe that this is society's greatest battle. It's all a load of lies.

Now listen, I am all for protecting the environment, and there are definitely real environmental issues happening in our world right now. Before I got into politics, I wanted to be a veterinarian for exotic big cats, so when I see the destruction of habitats and the extinction of animals across the world, I get incredibly concerned. I even work and volunteer with organizations to try to help because I want to see these magnificent animals and beautiful places on our earth survive and flourish. I even get called a hippie by other conservatives for doing this kind of stuff! But conservatives in general have gotten a bad reputation as the people who hate the climate and don't care about the environment, which couldn't be further from the truth. Let's look at history for a second, shall we? Conservatives, not the left, have been the dominant force behind conserving America's beautiful landscapes and wildlife. This first started in 1864, when Republican president Abraham Lincoln created the Yosemite Grant Act, which was the first act from the government to set aside land for public use. Next, in 1872, Republican president Ulysses S. Grant set up the first American National Park with Yellowstone. Then, in 1906, Theodore Roosevelt, another conservative president, signed the Antiquities Act, which gave power to the president to make national monuments. Then he made Devil's Tower in Wyoming the first national monument in America. Finally, in 1970, Richard Nixon, another Republican, helped get the ball rolling on the Environmental Protection Agency. Conservatives care about the climate, and rightly so, but to say that climate change is our biggest issue and that it is all we should be worried about is a total farce and distracts from the real environmental issues we should be worried about, and many of the solutions we see to protect the environment actually end up making things worse. The biggest culprit of this is renewable "clean" energy, specifically wind and solar.

Let's talk about solar energy first. Solar energy is first and foremost very destructive to the environment to make. The manufacturing of the panels creates an enormous amount of greenhouse gas from silicon. Silicon is first mined from quartz and then heated in a furnace to make it usable, which emits toxic sulfur dioxide and carbon dioxide into the atmosphere. The mining and transportation of the panels are also not good for the environment and cost a huge amount of energy to be completed. Then when solar panels need to be disposed of, the process is also incredibly difficult, costly, and environmentally unsafe. The toxic chemicals within solar panels cannot be disposed of easily and are a huge environmental concern. Solar industry leaders have come out and said that the disposal of solar panels will "explode in full force in two or three decades and wreck the environment." You might think that recycling them is a good solution, right? But in reality, according to a solar expert from China, "If a recycling plant carries out every step by the book, their products can end up being more expensive than new raw materials." So, since the recycling of the panels is so cost-ineffective, it makes it so that no company really wants to carry out the recycling in the first place.

For wind energy, the environmental impact is huge, especially on native wildlife populations. It is estimated that wind turbines kill anywhere from 140,000 to 328,000 birds every year. That's a lot of dead feathered friends that you would think these environmentalists would want to protect. Wind turbines also destroy the habitats and biomes where they are present, taking up huge amounts of land and adversely affecting the environment. Wind turbines, like solar panels, are also very hard to dispose of. The turbines have to be cut by a diamond saw into three parts to be able to be hauled away, and then the amount of greenhouse gas emitted trying to transport them is a lot on its own. Then the wind turbines end up in massive "windmill graveyards," where they take up huge amounts of land. Even if you burn the fiberglass turbines so they don't have to go in landfills, the toxins that go into the air can be just as environmentally unfriendly.

But many people when presented with this information will still say, "It's worth it," thinking that the costs don't outweigh the benefits. But in reality, they are missing the bigger picture. I would love if renewables like wind and solar could power America cheaply and efficiently, but it's just not the case. If we wanted to power the entire country with renewable energy, it would take 3 billion solar panels or 1.29 million wind turbines at a minimum with ideal conditions. To power the state of Texas with just wind and solar, you would need an area of land five times the size of Harris County, which contains the city of Houston and its surrounding suburbs and is a massive portion of land. If these environmentalists actually wanted to have a clean fuel source that was efficient, cheap, and abundant, they would turn away from wind and solar and look toward nuclear energy.

Nuclear energy first of all requires far less maintenance than alternatives, needing work only every 1.5 to 2 years. You would also need two coal plants or three to four renewable plants to produce the same amount of energy as one nuclear plant. The IPCC also reported that nuclear energy releases four times less carbon emissions than solar energy. A lot of people when citing nuclear energy as a bad fuel source claim that since the waste is toxic and can't be properly disposed of, it shouldn't be used. But in actuality, the waste can be stored safely, and if all the waste from the 1950s onward from nuclear energy was stored in the same place, it would only be the size of a football field with a depth of 30 feet. That same space is only a small fraction of the waste and land mass needed to dispose of all the material and components of so-called "green energy." Used nuclear fuel can also be recycled to make new fuel and different by-products, something that can't be said for the waste of renewables. And if that's not enough to convince the person you're talking to, a new study by the Dutch and Czech governments found that solar and wind energy require 148 to 536 times more land than nuclear energy and that they cost four times more than nuclear. The study also found that 100 percent of electricity from wind and solar would require an area of land 1.8 times larger than all of the Netherlands. In a myriad of ways, nuclear energy is a better alternative to green energy but has been demonized by the media and far-left activists in another effort to control the narrative.

When I have gone to the streets to interview and challenge people on climate change, I have been very successful with the right questions. I have really used many of the questions I'm about to show you in practice, and I have changed lots of people's minds with them. The first thing to do is to establish the stance of the person to whom you're talking. Do they think we only have 12 years left? Do they think there is a climate emergency? What do they think caused it? Once you find out where they stand on the issue, you can go into changing their mind on the topics. One thing we always hear from the media and far left is "the science is settled." I'm sure you have heard this before in regard to climate change. After you find out where the other person is at, ask them whether they think the science is settled. When they say yes, you can frame a lot of different questions. "If the science is settled, why are there more polar bears now than when Al Gore said they were all going to go extinct? If the science is settled, then why is there still snow on Mount Kilimanjaro? If the science is settled, then why are deaths from natural disasters going down, not up?" These questions make them question the experts' apocalyptic claims, and you can then follow up: "If all of these politicians and celebrities are so concerned with climate change and rising sea levels, why do they buy oceanfront property?" The key to this conversation isn't to make them flip their entire worldview on climate change; as I said in the beginning, this is a tough topic to change minds on at the first go, but what can be easily accomplished is making them lose faith in the people who profess the end of the world because of climate change. If they lose faith in the movement's leaders, then it is only a matter of time until they lose faith in the movement itself. You help light the match that changes their worldview, and then they figure out the rest with your help and the other information in this chapter.

Chapter 12

. . . .

SOCIALISM

OH, SOCIALISM. The magic buzzword that hundreds of thousands of young Americans love to echo as the savior of America. If only we implemented this one economic system, America would be a perfect place with no problems, no poor people, and no racism. All we need to do is listen to Bernie Sanders and all of our most vexing issues would be solved. People claim socialism is the future of America and that our capitalist society has failed to protect the individual. They think that Karl Marx's ideas actually protect the individual and take power away from the bourgeoisie and evil corporations and give it back to the worker. In short, most people, when asked to define socialism or explain what it means, say one thing: "Socialism means equality." This couldn't be further from the truth.

Socialism is the antithesis of "equality." Socialism

takes power away from the individual and gives it to the government. People hear socialism and think that the means of production are being taken away from the greedy business owner and given to the worker, but power is really just handed over to bureaucracy. Socialism is where the government owns the businesses, destroying private property and enterprise and putting the power in the hands of government employees. Advocates of socialism claim that this gives people freedom from the evil clutches of rich business owners, but all it really does is strip us of our freedom and destroy the free market. Let's look at a recent example through the timeline of the fall of Venezuela.

In the 1980s and early 1990s, Venezuela had an economy that was growing with access to education and healthcare and foreign trade, and above all else, it was a democracy. But in 1998, things were starting to change with the election of President Hugo Chavez. Chavez took much inspiration from Fidel Castro and told the people of Venezuela that "Venezuela is a nation of great wealth, but it's being stolen from its citizens by the evil capitalists and evil corporations." The three key things Chavez hoped to achieve with his socialist brand of "hope and change" were the nationalization of private industries, more spending on welfare programs, and currency and price control measures. And he did end up achieving these things. As he nationalized industries and taxed the rich to death, millions of people moved their money and businesses out of the country, and 2 million people left the country altogether. Eventually, there was no more money left for the government to take from corporations and rich individuals. The prices of basic goods started to skyrocket as they were in short supply, and crime exploded across the country. In 2016, it was shown that 75 percent of Venezuelan adults lost weight, as people weren't able to feed themselves or afford basic human goods. In 2013, the year Chavez died and was replaced by his vice president Nicolas Maduro, citizens were no longer allowed to buy guns, and people who opposed his rule or reported on the truth were jailed. Venezuela is a cautionary tale of what can happen when socialism takes over your country and people become so dependent on the government.

Many people will claim that Venezuela's story isn't "real socialism." I'm sure you've heard some leftist on your campus or on your social media timeline say that before. But the harsh reality is that what happened in Venezuela is real socialism; people just don't like to admit it. Socialism is a selfish system, where the government officials and bureaucrats have all the power and leave the people with nothing. When you take control of private industry, you don't liberate the people, you bind them. They can't set their own prices, they can't choose how much to pay their employees, and they can't budget their business. The government destroys the businesses and runs them into the ground when it gets control. One question I love to ask people when talking to them about socialism is "Have you ever been to the DMV?" They all say yes, and then you say, "It sucks, right? The employees are horrible and slow and don't really care about putting good work in." My listeners will surely agree because everyone knows the Department of Motor Vehicles is one of the most inefficient and terrible places to visit, and then you hit them with the closing question: "Imagine if your business was run by the same people who work at the DMV. Does that sound like a good idea?" They will always say no, and it's obvious why. When bureaucrats working off your tax dollars are in charge of something, they rarely are responsible or efficient. The great Milton Friedman said, "Nobody spends somebody else's money as carefully as he spends his own," and he is exactly right, especially when it comes to government employees who can just raise taxes and get more and more money from you. Government programs are incredibly inefficient and are never as successful as programs in the private sector.

At the beginning of this chapter, I stated that most people, when asked to define what socialism is, would say "equality." Now, most normal people wouldn't think of equality as such a bad thing. In fact, socialism does have a lot to do with equality in a broad sense, and equality can be a very good thing in many respects. But when it comes to socialism, equality is a perfect descriptor for what the left wants but not what the system achieves. It is true that socialism makes people equally poor, but it can't be real equality because the people in charge remain incredibly rich and powerful on the backs of the poor. Socialists believe in their brand of equality not because they want to give everyone a fair opportunity but because they can't stand the fact that some people are better off than others.

When I was a kid, I had a Game Boy Advance. My mom got me it for Christmas, and I was the happiest little boy in the world, sitting around playing Pokémon anytime I wasn't at school. But when I went to school, some of the other kids had the upgraded, newer system: the Nintendo DS. The Nintendo DS offered newer games and was a much better system than the Game Boy Advance I had. But when I saw the kids with the Nintendo DS, I didn't want to take their game system for myself. I was content with the games I had, and I wasn't envious of them for having a better system than me. That was just the way life was. But to the left, this would be a great atrocity. For someone to have something that

I didn't was totally unfair. If my teacher in school was a socialist, she would have taken the other boy's Nintendo DS and made him share it with me, even though that DS was not mine. She would have "redistributed the Nintendo DS" in the name of equality. This is why equality by redistribution through socialism doesn't work and is inherently selfish. Many people, even conservatives, when talking about socialism, say, "The ideas sound great on paper, but they will never work." But in reality, the ideas of socialism don't sound good on paper and actually sound incredibly selfish.

Socialism says there are rich or prosperous people who have more money than you and that you deserve their earnings. Of course, there are selfish, greedy, rich people who did cheat their way to get there, but this is the exception, not the rule. Socialism breeds laziness by telling people they don't need to work for something great; they can just take it from someone else. The people in charge say they are "redistributing" the wealth to make it fair for everyone, but really they are just giving themselves the power to do what they want with other people's money. This is why when people say, "That isn't real socialism," it isn't really correct because their view of socialism doesn't take into account human nature. When people are given power and other people's money, corruption always follows. This is why socialism will never work because when people have control over other people's money, there will always be deceit.

But some people claim, "Well, it's working in Nordic countries like Sweden and Denmark. Why can't it work in America? These are examples of successful socialist countries!" I'm sure you hear it everywhere from everyone you talk to about socialism and capitalism, that we should just be more like Nordic countries. The way they describe it makes it sound like a paradise where nothing ever goes wrong, a perfect example of socialism. The government takes care of its people, there's no corruption, and people get everything for free. This might be what people like Bernie Sanders, Alexandria Ocasio-Cortez, and the blue-haired girl in your sociology class try to tell you, but they're incredibly misinformed. They're wrong because Nordic countries are not successful examples of socialism. I mean, even after Bernie Sanders claimed Denmark was a socialist country, Danish prime minister Lars Lokke Rasmussen said, "I would like to make one thing clear, Denmark is far from a socialist planned economy. Denmark is a market economy." So how did so many people get it wrong? Why do so many people think Nordic countries are great examples of socialism when in reality they aren't? Well, let's look at what these countries' economies and systems are actually like and see why they're market economies and not socialist.

One of the main things that socialists like AOC push for in America is minimum wage requirements, which is funny because Sweden, Denmark, Iceland, and Norway have no minimum wage requirements. When we get to the chapter on minimum wage, I will explain this further, but this is an example of how the market sets the wages, not the government. It is a market-driven economy that doesn't need the government to tell people how to run their own businesses. Next, let's look at the tax rate in Nordic countries. In the 20th century after World War II, Sweden started to turn to more of a socialist model, with more regulations on businesses, state-owned companies, and higher tax rates. Many thought that these changes would further boost the country's economy, but they actually had the opposite effect. Sweden saw a sharp drop in innovation, and many businesses left the country. After 1990, Sweden enacted changes to make itself more of a free-market economy despite what Bernie Sanders would like you to believe. The country deregulated the market, companies owned by the government were sold, and competition in enterprise was able to flourish. Sweden cut taxes; got rid of property, inheritance, and gift taxes; and cut the size of government by a third. It implemented a school voucher program to give people even more freedom, all while creating more private jobs and more wealth. Bernie Sanders and AOC love to refer to these Nordic countries as socialist, but really they're referring to the past of these countries where people were poorer, there were fewer jobs, and the economy struggled. It was only when Sweden embraced capitalism and turned away from regulation and government control that it was actually able to flourish. If that's the socialism they are referring to, then sign me up!

Socialism is not alive and well in Nordic countries, and it has never worked anywhere it has been tried. If you look at the Economic Freedom Index put out by the Heritage Foundation, it shows that the countries that are the most socialist rank lowest in per capita income. The three lowest countries on this index are Cuba, Venezuela, and North Korea, and all are socialist. In comparison, the highest-ranked countries on that same index have income levels five times higher than those listed previously. That is because they are capitalist and have free markets. Everywhere socialism has been tried, people's lives have gotten worse, and in many cases, the countries have turned to communism and gotten exponentially worse. During the 20th century, socialism and communism killed 65 million people in China, 20 million in Russia, and 3.5 million in Korea and Afghanistan, and those are just a few examples. There are plenty of examples of places where socialism has been tried and has failed and people have died in massive numbers. Some people will counter you by saying, "That isn't socialism, that's communism, and I don't advocate for that." But this point couldn't have been addressed any better than by Vladimir Lenin himself, the man who led the socialist Russian Bolshevik revolution in the early 1900s, when he said, "The goal of socialism is communism." Socialism inevitably leads to communism because when people gain that level of power, it is incredibly difficult to slow down or give up. Communism is the end goal of socialism, and if you don't think it can happen here in America, you are sorely mistaken.

Some people you talk to will try to tell you that America is already socialist because we have state-funded police and fire departments and these are examples of socialism, but this couldn't be further from the truth. Just because something is funded by taxpayers doesn't make it intrinsically socialist; it just means it is taxpayer funded. Would the socialists really want to call President Trump a socialist because he gets a check for his salary from the government? Of course not. The police and firefighters and military are there to protect your *private* property and protect your God-given rights as an American and that is a legitimate role of government. Just because you aren't an anarchist that doesn't mean you're a socialist. We can all agree that the government has legitimate roles to which tax dollars should go to protect individuals and make our lives better, but when the things we pay taxes for infringe on our liberties or try to take away our private property, then we start getting into dangerous territory. It could be argued that America is headed in the direction of socialism with many of the policies and programs the left pushes through and advocates for, but that still doesn't mean every part of government is socialist. This is a trap that the left will use to pivot the argument away from the real issues of socialism and move toward trying to get a "Haha, got ya!" moment. Don't fall for their trap, and keep the discussion on point with all of the legitimate issues that real socialism brings.

I went to California State University, Los Angeles in the winter of 2019 to talk to people about socialism and change minds, and with the right information and explanation I was able to change everyone's way of thinking. I even had people afterward tell me they were now "anti-socialist" after speaking with me. This can be you if you ask the right questions and respond in the right way to their arguments. The first thing to do is to always know where your starting point is, so you should always ask them first to define what socialism is. This is where they may say equality or free healthcare or free college, and this is where you have the chance to explain to them what socialism really is, which is the government owning the means of production. After explaining to them what socialism really is or at least hearing what they think socialism is, then you can get into the meat of the conversation. Start by asking them if there are any successful examples of socialism, and they will most likely say Nordic countries. You then can go on to explain to them the information I presented earlier in this chapter about how Nordic countries are actually market economies with lower corporate taxes than America with a high social safety net and small populations. You then can ask them if there are any other examples they know of where real socialism has been tried and been successful. They probably won't have a great answer since there aren't any examples, and then you can ask them the final question: "If there are so many examples of failed socialist states and so many examples of successful capitalist ones, why would we want to continue trying a system that time and time again has failed?" All the other information in this chapter will help you answer any other questions that may come up, but the main point of all of it is that everywhere socialism has been tried, it has failed. Continue down that line of thinking and you will be able to change the mind of everyone you talk to about socialism.

Chapter 13

·············

"FREE" COLLEGE

A VIRAL VIDEO came out a couple years ago when Elizabeth Warren was running for president of the United States in the 2020 race. She was at a campaign event in Iowa when a father came up to her and started asking her questions about her stance on student loans. The father was visibly angry, pressing on her promise to cancel student loan debt if she was elected president. "My daughter is in school," he said. "I saved all my money just to pay my student loans. Can I have my money back?" Warren replied, "Of course not." He then responded again, saying, "So you want to help those who don't save any money and the ones that do the right thing get screwed? I saved my money. He made more than I did," he said, talking about another man he knew who spent his money poorly. "I worked a double shift, worked extra...so you're laughing at me."

She said, "No, I'm not," and he responded, "Yes, that's exactly what you're doing. We did the right thing, and we get screwed." It's funny; the people who talk the biggest game on this issue can't even defend their own positions rationally.

Right after our chapter on socialism we go straight to free college, another pinnacle of the leftist dream. Changing minds on free college is one of the easiest issues to talk to people about because the idea of it already makes no sense. Nothing in the world is free—everything has to be paid for by somebody—and so you are in some ways arguing against something that isn't even real. But alas, the left continues to push for this and make false promises, so we as conservatives have to continue to debate and convert people on the topic. Let's start with why people are talking about this in the first place.

First of all, young people nowadays are entitled. They feel like they are owed everything for free without having to work hard for it, and leftist politicians take advantage of this. They earn the vote of young people by promising them things they can't deliver on, like free college and free healthcare, and then get into power and earn clout, money, and influence. College gets more and more expensive, and leftists continue to preach how it should be free, enticing millions of people who have little knowledge of taxes and government. But how did college get so expensive in the first place? If college was cheaper, maybe people would not be calling for it to be free. The ironic thing about it is that the leftists who already work in our government are the reason why college is so expensive in the first place.

There is now over $1.6 trillion in unpaid student debt in America. That is more than credit card and auto loan debt, beat out only by mortgage debt. The reason why college is so expensive and so many people are in debt is because of government intervention. Once the federal government got involved with the student loan business, college started getting exponentially more expensive. Since 1978, the price of college has increased over 1,000 percent, way past the rate of inflation. Some tuitions can cost up to $50,000 a year, and students are able to afford this massive cost by taking out student loans. The average student in 2015 graduated with roughly $35,000 in student loan debt, and it takes the average student 10 to 20 years to pay off all their loans. Colleges continue to raise their prices, and the federal government continues to give bigger and bigger loans to incoming students, while the politicians and universities make money hand over fist, leaving students in massive debt. They do this by making interest off the student loan debt that people incur, and when it takes

20 years for a kid to pay off a loan, that's a lot of interest sent back to the government. Now imagine that millions of young people are taking out these loans and accruing huge amounts of interest on them. You also can't file bankruptcy on a student loan from the government, which means you will always be paying the government this money no matter what. This is why the colleges and government are working hand in hand to make college so expensive. Not because the quality of education is going up, but because they are making billions off the backs of the same college students they claim they are trying to help by giving them opportunity with such easily accessible loans. The colleges claim to be "helping" students by making student loans so easy to get, but in reality, they're all liars and are doing it for the sole purpose of getting filthy rich.

Back in the day, kids used to have to get good grades to get a student loan. Now it's basically a matter of not flunking out of high school and having a pulse and you'll get instantly approved. You used to have to have good grades, put on your best suit, and take your parents with you to the bank to cosign a student loan with you. It was much more difficult to get a loan, and you had to work hard in high school to be able to qualify. Now anyone can get a loan from the federal government, even if your grades sucked, because they want to make money off you. It doesn't matter if you fail out of college or have an emergency or decide you want to work instead of going to university; those loans through the government are with you forever. Again, you can't file bankruptcy on these loans, and so that debt carries with you forever. This system of quick approval for loans might seem like it would help lower-income students be able to get into school more easily or help kids who didn't have the best upbringing get into university, but in a lot of ways it makes things worse. A student who doesn't do very well in high school but is easily approved for a loan isn't going to do very well in college with the increased rigor in the classes, and so they will probably fail out. But even if they fail out, that student debt is still with them. We see the same thing with affirmative action policies, where many black and Hispanic kids with worse grades are admitted into school solely because of the color of their skin but fail out because the classes are too difficult. It's not that these kids are all stupid; it's just that they haven't been prepared to handle these harder classes by the education they had in high school. In America right now, only 59 percent of students exit college with a degree. That means that up to 41 percent of students who attended some college but didn't graduate will still have to pay off student loan debt. I am one of those students, and I am still paying off my student loans for two years of college in which I basically learned nothing of value. What a waste of money!

Now let's go back to the idea of making college "free" and the implications that would have on America. First of all, college is not "free"—hence the quotation marks. Someone still has to pay for it. The buildings have to be maintained, the resources and food and materials have to be paid for, the professors and staff all need salaries, and all of this requires a huge amount of money. No magical fairy comes down from the sky and pays for all of this; this is done through our tax dollars, and a lot of them.

First, we would have to repay 90 percent of the $1.6 trillion in student loan debt from the federal government, and then we would have to keep those taxes up to pay for all the new students going to school or people continuing their education. That is a lot of money, which means a lot more money out of your paycheck or your businesses bottom line to pay for it. Nobody wants to do that, and the people who want free college really don't understand the tax burden that will be laid on them if this leftist dream becomes a reality.

Second, if college did become totally taxpayer funded, where would the incentive be to go to school as quickly as possible or do your best with your education? Think about it. If you could just go to college without ever having to worry about the cost, wouldn't you borrow more? Wouldn't you take your sweet time in college rather than working hard? When you're given something for free, there is no incentive for you to treat it well. Imagine if someone gave you a car for free; knowing you could just get another one, how would you treat it? You would spill your coffee and leave it wet there on the seat. You would slam on the brakes and do donuts in the parking lot. You would push the pedal to the metal and floor it in a 35-mile-per-hour zone. Now imagine if you saved money and bought a car, knowing that you didn't have anymore money and this is the only car you would have. How would you treat that one? You would wash it regularly. You would take it in early for an oil change. You would drive the speed limit and keep it safe from harm. When people are given things for free with no repercussions, they never treat them well, and the same holds true for an education. Free college disincentivizes students from being patient and smart with their money and instead makes them reckless and uncaring, knowing that if they fail or do poorly, they can just do it again on someone else's dime.

Thirdly, just think for a second how unfair "free" college is to the average American. This goes back to the video with Elizabeth Warren I talked about at the beginning of the chapter and leads into what I think is the best question to ask when changing minds on this topic. Imagine you get out of high school and you don't want to go to college. You decide to start your own business instead, let's say a pizza company, and it starts to take off. You start making some cash, you hire more employees, and before you know it, you're making more money than a college graduate would. Then a leftist gets elected president and starts promising free college to everyone. Now you, a person who didn't graduate from college, have to pay taxes for other people to go to college for free. Then remember only 59 percent of people graduate from college, and the majority of people who do are getting degrees in communications and social sciences, degrees with high unemployment rates, and that you are paying for them to be able to go and do that. How screwed up is that? Imagine a trash man making $150,000 a year with no college degree now having to pay for someone else's college education for a gender studies degree. Nothing about that is fair, and people should have to be responsible for their own college degree, not have it paid for off the backs of hard-working Americans who decided college was not for them.

The idea of "free" college is a very stupid idea when you actually look at it fully. Aside from everything we have already talked about, making college free destroys the prestige of college. It turns college into a glorified high school when it is taxpayer funded, and since anyone will be able to go, the quality of the education will go down. Imagine there was a secret club that only a certain number of people who worked hard were able to get into, and then one day they just decided to let anyone into the club no matter their credentials. The club wouldn't be so elite and interesting anymore, would it? It would be filled with people who didn't work hard enough to get in with the old standards, and the quality of the club would go down. This is exactly what would happen to universities if they became free. Everyone would be able to go, and the overall prestige of having a college degree would go down even further, rendering it practically useless.

So, let's get into the questions to ask to actually change people's minds. First establish with your listener whether they think college should be free, and if they say yes, you move on to the next question. The first real question to ask deals with what we talked about earlier: being entitled to someone else's money. "If college was 'free,' that would mean it was taxpayer funded. Imagine if I chose not to go to college and get a job or start my own business. Why would someone else going to college to earn their degree be entitled to my money when I chose not to go to college myself?" This question deals with the real problem of this whole issue, which is the idea of freedom. People should be able to choose how to spend their money, not be forced to spend it on somebody else's higher education, which this question can help convince them of. I've found when I've asked this question that most people have never thought of it that way before and feel bad for making someone else pay for their education.

The second question to ask them is about the quality of education if college were free. You can ask, "If college were free, don't you think that would turn college into a glorified high school where everyone could get in? Wouldn't that ruin the prestige and honor of going to college in the first place?" Some people for this one may say no, so you can then continue on by pushing them about how people drop out when they aren't prepared for college. If everyone can get in, it only exacerbates the problem of people being unprepared and dropping out.

The last question to ask is the finisher to change their mind on the whole issue. Ask them, "If college was cheaper overall, would you be more willing to give up on the idea that college should be free? If it was cheaper, more people could pay for it, right?" They will agree, and you can then ask, "Do you know why college is so expensive in the first place?" They will say no, and then you can go on to explain to them what we talked about in the beginning of this chapter: how the colleges and government teamed up to make college expensive to keep kids hooked and make enormous amounts of money. If you can have a clear conversation with them sticking to this guide, you can easily change their minds on one of the most preposterous ideas the left tries to push.

Chapter 14

· · · · · · · · · · · ·

"FREE" HEALTHCARE

F REE COLLEGE, free healthcare, free the nipple. The left loves giving things away for free. If only they would apply that same attitude to capitalism and support free markets! Free healthcare is a lot like free college, where we see that we are debating an idea that doesn't make sense in the first place. Also, just like free college, nothing is free, and someone has to pay for it, which again would be the taxpayer. The difference between free healthcare and free college is that healthcare is much more important than college. Universities have become massive indoctrination centers and daycares in America, while healthcare is something that every single person uses and is necessary.

As you guys know, I grew up in Colorado, and whenever I tell people I'm from there, they love to tell me all about how great the 303's weed is. I hate that my home state is stigmatized with that, but alas, that's how it is. Because of this love of marijuana in Colorado, every April 20, there is a massive 4/20 festival celebrating the drug, and so in 2019 I went to shoot a video. I decided to make it about free healthcare and ask the stoners and celebrators what they thought about it, and the answers I got were exactly what you'd expect. When asked if they wanted free healthcare, they all said yes. When asked who would pay for it, they all said, "I don't know." Many of them felt like they should get weed for free as well but, again, had no idea who was going to pay for it. This is the main point to address regarding "free" healthcare. Everyone thinks they deserve something for free and that they are entitled to it. There is a lot of information to debate people on when it comes to this topic and how to change minds, but the main thing to keep in the back of your mind is that you have to convince people to feel less entitled. If you do that, you can easily get them to understand that free healthcare isn't really free and that it is not the best way to handle our current healthcare system.

Every time I talk to leftists on this issue, whether that's on campus, on social media, or at debates, I hear one line over and over again: "Healthcare is a human right." I'm sure you've heard it before too. This little quip is a way to shut down any argument you have on the topic. It puts you in a position where no matter how expensive, how inefficient, how troublesome getting universal healthcare is, it is necessary, and everyone is entitled to it. Let's break this down so you can adequately combat this point before moving on to the rest of the argument.

First, healthcare is much too broad a topic to define in the one word "healthcare." What does that really mean? Is it clean water so everyone can stay healthy? Is it vaccines so you don't get sick? What about lifesaving surgeries? Or what about check-ins with your doctor about a sore back? Or therapy sessions with a psychiatrist? Or maybe you want a boob job—how about that? All these things could fit under the wide umbrella of "healthcare," but what is actually necessary and what isn't? If you are talking to someone about healthcare being a human right, it is important to press them on this and get their definition of what healthcare actually is. Some might say therapy is not necessary to be covered in a universal healthcare system because it is only mental health and your life isn't in danger, while some people might say without therapy someone could kill themselves or hurt others, so it is incredibly necessary. The line for this is very gray, and you and the person you're talking to need to get on the same common ground moving forward in the rest of the chat.

Second, let's talk about the main problem with universal free healthcare, which is you being entitled to someone else's labor. Imagine you are a doctor doing surgeries in a free-market system. When people need surgery, they come to the hospital and pay for the surgery through cash or their own health insurance, and you perform it. It is a mutual transaction, and both people benefit. Now imagine if you are in a free healthcare system as that same doctor. Essentially you are a government employee, and the government is now paying for the surgery. This also means that people are *entitled* to your labor. The government gets to choose the price of the surgery and how much to pay you for it, and you just have to do it. You could quit, but you wouldn't be able to be a doctor anymore, since in the public healthcare system there would be no private practices. What this means is that people's "right" to healthcare is totally dependent on you, the doctor, meaning that the only way for *them* to have their human right is for *you* to work for them. This is why you cannot have a human right that is based on someone else's labor. Someone else is responsible to provide you with that human right, and that is a total restriction of their freedom of choice.

Let's look at an example of government-run healthcare in the United States: the system at Veterans Affairs. Back at the 4/20 march in Colorado, I talked to a man who was actually a veteran. When asked about free healthcare, he said we need to "get into the 21st century" like the other countries around the world that already have universal healthcare. But then when I asked him about the VA as an example of failed government care, he completely agreed. He said he had been waiting seven months for an appointment and that the government made a mess out of the VA. If you give people real examples of failed American government care, you can open up their minds instead of just having them base their feelings on examples from countries far away that they know nothing about. To put it simply, the VA does not work well. If you don't know what the VA is exactly, it is a government agency that provides healthcare services to military veterans. There are 1,700 medical centers and clinics across the country that specialize in healthcare and some healthcare-related specialties for American veterans. With the government involved in the VA, that means the government hires the doctors and staff and owns the medical facilities. It may have a lot of clinics and facilities for veterans, but the VA is not run well. This is what happens when the government runs your healthcare. The wait times at many of these centers are horrible, and veterans are not able to get the care they need.

In Phoenix, Arizona, three VA healthcare officials

were put on leave after as many as 40 patients died after delays in treatment. Records of patients were also hidden so people wouldn't know the number of patients who weren't being treated (none were charged with crimes relating to patient deaths or records). In Colorado, records were falsified, and veterans had to wait months to get the care that they needed. The bureaucracy within the VA is insane, and this is the result of having your system run by the government. Medical equipment, practices, and prescriptions are outdated, and there are plenty of stories from veterans describing things that were done at the VA that would never happen in a private hospital with updated technology.

These problems aren't because of a lack of funding, either, as from 2009 to 2015, the VA budget grew over 58 percent and is continuing to rise. The VA needs a massive overhaul, and the best thing to do would be to give the veterans vouchers where they can choose the best care for themselves in the private sector and aren't forced to go to the terrible VA clinics throughout America filled with scandal and bureaucracy. Veterans need more freedom with their healthcare, not more government control, and this is a clear example of what happens when you get the government involved in people's healthcare.

But what about Canada? When I talk to leftists about free healthcare, they always say, "Canada has free healthcare. We should be more like Canada!" Well, how does Canada's healthcare system even work? First of all, Canada's "universal" healthcare actually only covers about 70 percent of all medical costs, leaving out some pharmaceuticals, dental, and vision. Even with this lack of coverage, Canadian households still pay over $9,000 a year on average for their healthcare. So much for "free," huh? To keep costs down, Canada, like the VA, still uses outdated equipment and medicine; Canada has fewer MRI machines per capita than Turkey. Wait times in Canada's system are also terrible, with wait times for the ER over four hours long in some cases. Seeing specialists can also take a long time.

Here is one story from the Heritage Foundation: "One doctor in Ontario called in a referral for a neurologist and was told there was a four-and-a-half-year waiting list. A 16-year-old boy in British Columbia waited three years for an urgent surgery, during which his condition worsened, and he was left paraplegic. One Montreal man finally got the call for his long-delayed urgent surgery—but it came two months after he had died." To escape these long wait times, Canadians come to America, the same place leftists who live here want to turn into Canada. Ironic, isn't it?

Canadian hospitals and clinics aren't able to upgrade their equipment and have such long wait times because they are all price rationed. What this means is that doctors and administrators have to budget their spending to an incredibly tight degree set by the government. The hospitals are forced to ration their care so they don't overspend, which in turn gives them outdated equipment and technology and incredibly long wait times. They can't upgrade their equipment, and they can't see every patient in a timely manner, or they will go over budget. This is what happens when the government sets the prices and standards for your care, and there is no freedom of choice from the doctors and hospitals. Canada's healthcare system has raised taxes, made the treatment worse, and totally increased the wait times and is the exact opposite of what America should be looking to as an example.

After you talk about Canada, I'm sure that they will bring up a myriad of other examples of places where "free" healthcare works. The UK, Sweden, Finland, Denmark—you name it, there are lots of examples of countries with socialized medicine. You could write a whole book going through all of them and their inefficiencies and the differences in their systems, but there is one thing they all have in common. They all depend on America. If you want cutting-edge technology, low wait times, and the best care, America is the place to go. People from America are not going to the UK or

Canada for care; the people from those countries are coming to America. The reason these countries are able to even have a shot at their universal healthcare models is because of the United States. The United States spends way more than any of these other countries on medical research and new technologies, and over $70 billion per year of this research and development is spent in the private sector. Due to the fact that America has a free-market healthcare system where finding new medical technologies can be an extremely profitable business, the rest of the world profits off our innovation and reaps the benefits of our new technology and research. In short, without America, these other countries' universal systems would never be possible.

What about the cost? How much would it really cost to have a free healthcare system in America like Bernie Sanders wants? According to a Mercatus study, a free healthcare system in America would cost the amount of money we already spend on healthcare now plus another $32.6 trillion over 10 years. I'll say it again—$32.6 trillion. According to the author of the Mercatus study, even if you doubled all corporate and income taxes in America, it still would not be enough to pay the incredible cost of government healthcare in America. Doesn't sound so "free" now, does it? All the people who think free healthcare is the way forward and is the way to make their lives better are totally misguided by the way the left describes it. Universal healthcare is not free in any way, shape, or form, and by using the word "free," the left is able to manipulate millions of Americans into thinking it is the way America should be.

So how do we change minds on free healthcare with the best questions? The first thing to do is to establish that healthcare provided by the government is not free. Ask, "Who pays for the free healthcare?" They either will not know or will say taxpayers. If they say they don't know, you simply have to tell them it is they who have to pay for it. Then you tell them the enormous burden it would be on the taxpayers and how much it would actually cost from the preceding data. Again, the main thing we have to get across to people is that free healthcare *is not* free. I know I keep bringing this up, but it is paramount that whomever you are talking to understands it. Nothing is free, and it always has to be paid for by somebody.

At this point in the conversation, you can start getting into the VA and other countries' healthcare systems, as I'm sure they will bring them up. You can bring these things up as well by asking questions and not just telling them. You can ask, "Do you think that Canadian healthcare is efficient?" or, "Do you know why the VA is so horrible?" and then go on to explain the reality to them based on their answers.

"FREE" HEALTHCARE

The last part of this debate is the fairness aspect. Just like free college, the issue of whether someone should have to pay for someone else's healthcare is a very important question but is a little different with healthcare versus college. Many people would argue that healthcare is much more important than college and should be taxpayer funded. While it is true that healthcare is much more necessary in most cases than college for the majority of people, the issue of fairness is still there. You can ask a person you're talking to this: "Imagine I am a very healthy individual. I have a good job, provide for my family, and save my money. I never smoke, I never drink, I work out, and I eat a lot of healthy food. Now imagine you are a very unhealthy person. Let's say you're actually an alcoholic and you decide to get behind the wheel of a car and drive. You end up crashing into a tree in your drunken stupor and totally destroy your body. You were a drunk and had no money, but because of free healthcare, you now get medical treatment paid for by taxpayers. Is that fair that I, a healthy, hardworking individual, now have to pay for the healthcare of someone else who made the conscious decision to put their own life in danger and drink and drive? Or what about a lifelong smoker? Should I have to pay for their medical treatment as well, even though they knew the consequences of what smoking

211

can do? Why would people with good medical histo-
ries and lots of money need to pay for the medical care
of unhealthy individuals?" This question may sound a
little heartless, I know, like, are we supposed to just let
the people die? Of course not; that is ethically and morally wrong. But to think that some other individual has
the responsibility to pay for someone else is also wrong.
In a free-market system where people can freely choose
their own insurance and hospitals, and doctors can set
up their own payment plans and prices, these kinds of
questions don't need to be answered. In a socialist universal healthcare system, all these moral dilemmas will
come up constantly, and it will be the healthy individuals paying for the people who made unhealthy choices.
People's minds can be changed on this issue by convincing them it isn't free, other systems don't work and only
have the illusion of working because of American innovation, and people should have personal responsibility
to pay for their own healthcare. If you can convince
them on those three things, you will always change
their minds on the idea of free healthcare.

Chapter 15

· · · · · · · · · · · ·

MINIMUM WAGE

'VE HAD A lot of jobs. Before working as the political commentator I am now, I did various other things. I was a lifeguard, field director, burrito maker, camp counselor, check-in boy at the gym, landscaper, fence repair guy, pizza boy, dog watcher, server, and even male nanny. Ever since I was 14, I have been working at one job or another, and over that time I worked for a lot of different wages. Sometimes I just got cash from whoever hired me, sometimes I worked pretty much just for tips, and sometimes I got minimum wage. Most kids growing up have had some sort of minimum wage job at some point through high school or college, and those types of jobs are a great stepping-stone to what life would become. You do those jobs to gain work experience and learn responsibility and time management, and if you do them well, you get advancement. But the left, with the push to raise the minimum wage, treats those types of jobs like they are people's careers. Now I understand that not everyone is going to have some crazy, nice salary job, but it is still also true that minimum wage jobs are not meant to be for life. The minimum wage is a policy from leftists that sounds really nice and good on paper but is actually extremely harmful and destroys businesses and people's self-worth.

The minimum wage first came about in America in Massachusetts in 1912 with a 38-cent-an-hour minimum wage. Then in 1938, Congress passed the Fair Labor Standards Act, which mandated a national minimum wage of 25 cents an hour. In 1949, the wage was raised to 75 cents per hour, and in 1963, President Kennedy passed the Equal Pay Act, which gave people from all groups the same pay for the same work. In 1968, the federal minimum wage was raised again to $1.60, which would be about $11.53 per hour when adjusted for inflation for today. As of 2019, 29 states and Washington, D.C., have higher minimum wages than the federal requirement, and many states are pushing for even higher. Increases to the minimum wage have always been met with great applause from progressives and politicians, but economists are too smart to fall for the trap. Nearly 75 percent of economists oppose the minimum wage, and for good reason; everywhere it is implemented it makes things worse.

MINIMUM WAGE

Let's look at why politicians would want to push for a higher minimum wage in the first place. The minimum wage, like welfare in a way, is something that people get dependent on. There are 1.7 million people in America who work minimum wage jobs and 60 million people who depend on the minimum wage, including 15 million children. For politicians, that is a huge voting bloc. When they think of those 1.7 million people, they don't think these people need more opportunity and more freedom with their wages; they think, "Hey, I could get all these people to vote for me!" Imagine you're a young politician coming on the scene and running for some office, and you toe a classic fiscally conservative line. Your platform states you want to get rid of the minimum wage, while on the other side of the aisle, your opponent tells people they want to raise it to "help the little guy." Now imagine you're a voter in this district and you have a minimum wage job or imagine you don't know much about economics or only have a high school diploma. Which person are you going to vote for? Of course, the person who promises to raise your wages. This is another example of the left promising something that is supposed to help people when in reality it does the opposite and only serves to give them more power. And, of course, all these politicians make tons of money when they get elected, and none of them are in need of a minimum wage job. Politicians use raising the minimum wage as a way to get votes from lower-class and younger voters by promising them more money, but in reality in the long run, it only ends up making everybody poorer.

So, we talked about why people are pushing for a higher minimum wage, but what actually happens when you do raise it? Let's talk about a basic scenario. Imagine you own a small business, and you have three employees. Each one makes $10 an hour, and each one is happy with their wage at the moment. Paying them $10 an hour is all you can do as a business owner without making yourself go broke, but since your employees accepted the job of their own volition, it is all good. Now imagine the government comes in and says you have to pay your employees a $15 minimum wage. What does that mean for you? Well, you can't afford to pay each one an extra $5 an hour, so you have to let one of them go. Now you have two employees working for the same amount of money as when you had three employees, and in turn, your business suffers. You are one person short for the work you need done but are still having to pay the same amount of money out in wages, and eventually your business shuts down. This is what happens when you raise the minimum wage. It is a temporary boost to *some* employees' earnings in the short run, but in a short amount of time, both business owners and employees suffer the consequences.

Seattle is a perfect case study of what happens when you actually raise the minimum wage. In 2014, Seattle voted to increase the minimum wage to $15 over a seven-year time period. A study by the University of Washington found that in 2016 the increase in wages reduced work hours for low-wage jobs by around 9 percent on average, resulting in a net loss of $125 per month per person. This is bad news for everyone. Not only does it make low-wage workers lose money in the long run because employers have to cut hours, it changes the ways employers have to run their businesses. Luckily when I was a lifeguard, there was no way to replace my job with some autonomous robot that could do my job for me more efficiently and for free. But in a lot of businesses, robots and technology are the future.

Imagine you're the CEO of Target and the government raised the minimum wage. What do you do? Do you take it on the chin and take the losses in profit to help your employees, or do you figure out how to make it cheaper and turn this scenario into a win? The answer is obvious, and that's what thousands of businesses have decided to do. Instead of hiring new employees or giving more hours to the ones they have, they lay off employees and replace them with new technology.

In Target's case, that would be self-checkout machines. Self-checkout machines mean that employees don't have to be present to ring you up for your goods, and thus employees aren't needed. It saves the company money but in turn demands that people be let go to make room for the new machines. At a fast-food restaurant like McDonald's or Chick-fil-A, they now have self-ordering stations where people no longer have to see a cashier; they can just order on the machine. When the government raises wages through the minimum wage, businesses don't first and foremost think of ways to save their employees; they think of ways to lower their operating costs to make more money, and automation is the future. Now this isn't necessarily a bad thing. The free-market innovation in business to make companies more successful and the customer experience better is a good outcome, but regardless of all that good, the consequences on the person looking for low-wage work are real. Businesses are not charities, they are businesses, and they are always going to be worried about the bottom line to keep their businesses open.

With all that said, it should come as no surprise that minimum wage hikes affect low-skilled, less-educated people the most. When I was 16, no matter how many lives I wanted to save or what kind of good I wanted to do, I could not be a doctor, so I had to take a low-wage, entry-level position as a lifeguard instead. I was a low-skill worker, and I didn't have much of a choice but to take a job that didn't require much experience. This is also the case for millions of other Americans. Whether you're a teenage kid looking for a job, a high school dropout, someone with a criminal record trying to get back on your feet, or someone with some other circumstance preventing you from becoming a highly skilled worker at the moment, minimum wage increases hurt you, not help you.

At a time when minimum wage laws weren't so high or in states with less aggressive minimum wage laws, low-skill workers were able to get jobs much more easily because these entry-level positions didn't cost business owners as much. But once the minimum wage rises, these low-skill jobs now have to be paid at a much higher wage, forcing businesses to not want to hire low-skill workers because if they're shelling out more money per employee, they want the best worker they can get. Thus, less-skilled and less-educated workers no longer have good entry-level job positions available for them, and they struggle to find work. This is what happens to thousands of families and individuals across the nation when the minimum wage increases. The same people who these programs are supposed to help actually end up being hurt by them in the long run. Talk about counterintuitive.

I went to UCLA and asked students how high the minimum wage should be, and this showed that these students had never heard anything like the stuff I had talked about throughout this chapter. I first started by asking students how high the minimum wage should be overall. Most said $15 or around there, and then after that, I raised the wages. I asked if $25 was a good wage, and they said yes. Then I asked if $35 was good, and they said yes. Then $45 an hour and so on until they caught on to what I was doing. They then would realize how arbitrary the number was and that the number could continue to rise to no end. I asked this question not to fool the students but to show them how out of control the minimum wage can be. The politicians can continue to promise higher and higher wages, and people will continue to vote for them and increase because they don't understand the economics behind the situation.

This is a great way to get into a conversation with someone about minimum wage: by asking them how high the minimum wage should be and then raising the number until they say it shouldn't be higher than that.

After that you can get into more of the meat of the conversation. Next, you can ask them about Seattle: "Did you know Seattle raised the minimum wage? Do you know what happened there?" Unless they are from

Seattle, they probably won't know, and even if they are from Seattle, they still probably won't know. This is where you can explain to them the net loss of income from raising the minimum wage and how it negatively affected employees and laborers alike.

After this, you can get into the hypotheticals we talked about earlier in the chapter: "Did you know most businesses run at an average profit margin of 7 percent? With already so little room for increased costs, how do you think a business is supposed to stay open when the government forces it to pay employees more? Don't you think it would have to let people go or eventually close down if it had to pay employees a wage set by the government?"

You can also ask them about how it would affect low-skill workers: "If you had a business and had to pay employees a higher amount, wouldn't you defer from hiring low-skilled workers and look to only hire people with more experience?"

A good tip for all the topics in this book and all the questions you ask is to put the person you're talking to in the shoes of whomever you're talking about. If you're talking about minimum wage, put them in the shoes of the business owner who now has to let someone go because of increased wages. This strategy makes them think about what they would do in that situation, not just arbitrarily with some random person in the world, and gets them connected to the issue. For any topic you talk to people about, this is a great way to change their mind.

The last thing to ask is about prices: "Imagine you're the owner of a restaurant, for example. If the government raises the minimum wage, won't you have to raise the prices in your restaurant to keep up with the higher wages? Isn't that bad for business and the economy at large?" All of these things are common-sense economics when you really think about them, and after you ask the right questions, putting your listener in the shoes of the business owner, they will easily wake up to the fact that raising the minimum wage is a terrible idea for not just businesses but employees as well.

Chapter 16

. . . .

CAPITALISM

THE WORD "CAPITALISM" is seen as a dirty word in America nowadays. Leftists and misinformed Americans don't use the word as a way to describe an economic system; they use it as a way to describe evil. Capitalism by their definition equals greed and malice and is used as a means to crush the little guy and get filthy rich. They think capitalism is the worst thing to ever happen to America and the west and that it has to be replaced by a new system. The funny thing is that when people describe it this way, they are missing the whole point. Capitalism can be described really in one sentence: Capitalism is the mutual transactions between people. Does that sound so bad or so evil? Of course not, and that is the clear definition of what capitalism is. Capitalism when implemented in a society turns into much more than that, but at the heart of it, even in a country with millions of people, that is the basis for what it is: millions of people making transactions through their own discretion for things they want or need.

When I went to California State University, Los Angeles to ask people about capitalism, I was shocked at how little the students knew about it. I essentially had to explain it to them like they had never heard of it before. I gave them a situation. Imagine you have a sandwich, and I have $5. You, wanting my $5, and me, wanting your sandwich, decide to make a transaction in which I give you my $5 and you give me your sandwich. It is that simple. Capitalism is the voluntary exchange of goods or services for something else, and humans have been doing it for thousands of years. Capitalism is what has made society flourish and the human race so successful because people have traded with each other and more wealth is created.

Again, imagine you are the same guy with a sandwich. You find that you can make the sandwiches for $4 but can sell them for $5. Eventually you save the money you make from the sandwiches you're selling, and you hire another guy to help you make sandwiches. Then you can sell double the sandwiches and make more money. Then eventually you can open up another store, hire more people, and make more and more sandwiches for people who want to buy them. The left says that this system of capitalism is exploitative and takes advantage of people, but with a pure capitalist sense, how does it do that at all? No one is forcing other people to buy the sandwiches from you, and no one is forcing you to make the sandwiches. If your sandwiches are bad or overpriced, people won't buy them, and so you have to make a good product for it to be purchased. Capitalism in its original intent is totally voluntary, and both the person selling the sandwiches and the person buying them benefit.

This sandwich situation is only one hypothetical example of what happens millions of times per day across the world. You buy a coffee, you fill up your gas tank, you buy a new barbecue grill, you sell a mattress online—all of these are examples of what capitalism is, and capitalism has the power to bring millions of people out of poverty. In fact, capitalism is the only way to bring people out of poverty despite what the left would have you believe about how evil it is.

Let's look at Chile. Chile is a country with a complicated past that has gone through many changes in a short period of time. It was first controlled by Marxists in the early 1970s but had a big change to a more militaristic government in the late 1970s. Some problems definitely took place when Augusto Pinochet took power in Chile, including human rights violations, but in an economic sense, Chile began to flourish, and by 1990, it was a democracy. In the 1980s, Chile began to institute economic free-market reforms; between 1973 and 2019, the Chilean economy grew by 293 percent, and it has the highest GDP per capita in any country in South America. Mortality rates for children declined, people got access to better healthcare, people started to live longer, and now Chile is ranked as having the 15th freest economy in the world. These free economy and capitalist properties are what made Chile such an economic powerhouse. The socialist policies it instituted beforehand are what set it into a world of chaos in the first place, and only capitalist principles got it to be a free, flourishing economic triumph.

Capitalism hasn't just been successful in helping Chile; it has been successful in helping people all over the world. The number of people living in extreme poverty has gone down by 80 percent from 1970 to 2006, all thanks to capitalism. In 1820, 94 percent of the world's population was in poverty, and by 1983, that number was 53 percent. By 2011, that number had declined even further to only 17 percent. Once again, because of capitalism. From 1988 to 2008, people in the lower and middle classes saw a 40 percent increase in wages. Can you guess how? If you guessed capitalism, you're right! Child mortality rates also went down 49 percent from 1990 to 2013, according to the World Health Organization. With the free market, children and mothers around the world get better access to medicine and treatment, producing an all-around higher standard of living. Capitalism is the key to bringing the world out of poverty, and right now because of capitalism, the world has the lowest number of people living in poverty than ever before.

The ironic part about all the hate on capitalism is that the same people who hate on it benefit from it every day. When I went to the University of San Diego and asked people about Che Guevara and their "Che Cafe," I got into it with one guy who said Che Guevara was a socialist icon and that socialism was the best future for America. I then asked him where he bought his clothes. He was perplexed at first but answered that he got them at a thrift store. I then asked him if he had an iPhone, to which he replied yes. I then was able to ask him if he knew how all the products he wore and used were created. He didn't know exactly, but the main point I made to him is that all those things—his thrift shop clothes, his iPhone, and his little nose ring—were all products of capitalism. Someone in the free market made goods that he wanted to purchase, and with the money he had from a job or his parents or whatever else, he was able to buy that good of his own volition. No one was forcing him to buy the products he had, and he did so because he wanted to. If he lived under socialism, the government would own the industry and get to set the prices. The business does not get to choose how much to sell its nose rings for, the government does, and thus you can't shop around or find the best deal or find the one you like; you are forced to choose from one place. With capitalism there is endless variety when there is demand, and there is no other economic system that provides that type of variety and innovation except for capitalism.

Let's look at the Trump administration for a moment and see how it made America more capitalist with less government control, and the effects that had. The Trump administration cut taxes and deregulated the market, and in return America saw amazing growth in the economy. Minority groups had some of the lowest unemployment rates seen in generations, and people's personal buying power increased. In the first three years of Trump's administration, before the COVID pandemic hit, the median household income increased to $68,703 per year. This was an increase of $5,800 per year, or a 9 percent total increase since 2016. This is a big bump and never would have been possible without the help of capitalist principles implemented in the Trump economy.

This same plan of deregulation and tax cuts was

seen first in the Reagan administration in the 1980s, where the economy once again did extremely well after a rough spot in the 1970s because of free-market economic practices with limited government intervention. Reagan cut the top income tax rate from 70 percent to 28 percent over his eight years in office and also cut the top corporate tax rate from 48 percent to 34 percent. During his eight years as president, Reagan created 16.5 million jobs due to these tax cuts and deregulation efforts, the second highest increase in jobs by any president and also the second highest percentage of jobs created by any president. Reaganomics, as it has been dubbed by economists, did have its problems, but when looking at the Reagan administration and the Trump administration, it is clear to see that more capitalism, not less, is a key to successfully creating a stronger, self-sustaining economy.

All this stuff about capitalism saving lives and helping people get access to healthcare and strengthening the economy sounds great, so why do people talk down about capitalism so much if all that is true? The first reason is that people are envious. Socialists are envious. They see what successful people have in their lives that they worked hard for, and they want to take it from them. Capitalism is freedom, and with that freedom, some people have the ability to get very rich if people really like what they have to sell. People see that wealth created and think that is a terrible thing, thinking, "Why does this person deserve to have all this money and be better off than me?" This is a very selfish attitude to have and is the attitude many anti-capitalists have. They see what another man has and has worked for, and they covet instead of thinking how they can create that same wealth for themselves.

The important part when talking to people about this is to ask them, "Okay, yes, one man can get very rich because of capitalism, but does that inherently make someone else poorer? Because the CEO of Walmart is very rich and made millions and millions of dollars, did that make anyone else lose money?" Walmart itself started as a small business by one man, Sam Walton, in 1962 with its first store but has since exploded into a massive chain of stores. With the creation and success of Walmart, millions of jobs were created, and billions of dollars were brought into the economy. Yes, the people who started Walmart became incredibly rich, but the world benefited from this, and people did not become poorer because the Waltons got rich; in fact, people got wealthier. Just because someone else got rich does not mean someone else got poorer, and in almost all cases, people get more money because of this. Instead of demonizing stores like Walmart, capitalist haters should be happy that Walmart came in and revolutionized the way stores do business forever and made millions of people money by providing millions of products at a great price. People are envious of the CEO of Walmart because he has tons of money, but because of all this money, people are able to see Walmarts all over where they can cheaply get the goods and services they use every day.

The second, and more difficult to explain, reason why people don't like capitalism is because of the phenomenon known as crony capitalism. Crony capitalism is where businesses lobby the government and get special treatment. This is why we see some businesses getting so massive and shutting out all competition because they take advantage of the government by paying it off. The government is bought off by a business paying it to buy its products, and thus competition in the free market is destroyed. People in Congress get filthy rich by doing this, lining their own pockets from corporate interests and snuffing out the competition in certain businesses' favor. This is a valid reason to hate big business, and I get a lot of flak from conservatives for even talking about this, but it really is something the left and right should come together to put a stop to. The reason why some conservatives get mad at me for this is because, first, they think capitalism is the be all and end all and don't think the government should be involved and, second, Republicans in government are just as guilty in this as the Democrats, so they don't want to talk about it. I will go more into this issue in the final chapter of this book, but just know how to spot the difference between crony capitalism and real capitalism so when you talk to people about how evil capitalism is you can explain to them the difference and agree with them that the crony version should be stopped.

Capitalism is a hard topic to change people's minds on because of the fierce correlation capitalism has with negative thoughts in people's minds, but with the right questions and the right lines of reasoning, you can definitely change their minds on the issue and at the very least inspire them to do their own research on it. The first thing you need to do is to have them define capitalism. As with all the topics in this book, it is always a good idea to ask the person with whom you're talking to describe what you are talking about in a nonconfrontational way. Don't ask in a rude way like you're expecting them not to know; ask in a way that shows you are looking for an actual genuine answer. If you can both come to an agreement on the definition of whatever you're talking about, it makes it much easier for you to have a productive discussion; otherwise you both will just be arguing in circles about definitions and semantics, which in the end gets you both nowhere.

CAPITALISM

If they don't know what capitalism is, the best thing you can do is to explain to them the sandwich situation we talked about in the beginning of this chapter and have them understand that before going any further. As we've talked about in this chapter as well, capitalism is the greatest system ever devised to lift people out of poverty. A great question to ask people is "Do you know any system other than capitalism that has raised millions of people out of poverty?" They will probably not know or say Scandinavian countries' socialism (which, as we discussed in the chapter on socialism, is actually capitalism), and then you can get into all of capitalism's successes. "Did you know that capitalism brought Chile out of extreme poverty into democracy after socialism? Did you know that the world is 120 times better off today than in 1800 because of capitalism? Did you know that child mortality rates fell 49 percent from 1990 to 2013 because of capitalism?" You can use these examples as well as the other ones we talked about in this chapter to show the sheer power capitalism has had in making the world a better, freer, and more prosperous place.

If they are still not convinced after this, you can ask them about themselves: "If you don't like capitalism, why do you support and use products every day that are the products of capitalism? Do you have an iPhone? Do you have unique clothes? Do you have a car? You are only able to buy all of these goods because of the free market and capitalism giving you the best value for your money and the greatest variety in a competitive market. Do you think you'd be able to get these same prices and this selection of goods and services in a socialist system?" This is definitely more of an aggressive question to ask people, so don't be shocked if, at this point, they get more defensive. Be ready to bring the conversation back to a civil and productive place if it gets out of hand and move on to the last question.

At this point, if you both haven't come to an agreement, they will probably be talking about how capitalism takes advantage of poor people and only caters to the rich. You can finish with this: "Wouldn't you say capitalism actually helps poor people because it helps give them an opportunity to get out of poverty by either starting a business or using their skills as a valuable employee? Without capitalism, what opportunity would these people have to start a new life or build themselves up financially?" This is where the conversation should end because there is no other system besides capitalism that can bring massive amounts of people out of poverty. Socialism can't, and if these people really cared about poor people, they would be looking for less government control and more free markets, not the opposite.

Chapter 17
. . . .

A VISION FOR AMERICA

WHAT IS A real conservative's vision for America? I'm not just talking about conservative talking points and ideas, but what our actual plan is. I'm not talking about the Republican Party platform or something that the politicians promise. I'm talking about the real proposal conservatives need to put forward to save this country. I ask this to lots and lots of conservatives all the time, and no one seems to have a great answer. Most of the answers I hear are just a pushback against big government blandly or a push against the left or against the liberal media, but all these plans have one thing in common: They are all defensive. Conservatives for far too long have taken the defensive position, only putting forward plans and visions that are a direct answer to what the left is already doing. But by the time that conservatives develop a plan or talking point

241

or call to action to combat the latest leftist agenda, it is too late, and the left's plan has already come to fruition. Conservatives have to get off the defensive and on the attack to push our ideas forward, instead of everything we believe in being against whatever the left is saying at the time. We also have to rethink our messaging and get rid of many of the same old stale talking points we have been using for years.

One thing we hear conservatives reference all the time is how bad Venezuela is. It is true—don't get me wrong, socialism ruined that country, and it is a good example of what a tyrannical government can do to your country—but saying, "Venezuela is bad" is not a vision for America; it is only a defense on what the left already got away with. I've never been to Venezuela, and almost everyone else I know has never been to Venezuela, so it is hard to get people to connect with it. We also see lots of conservatives today saying platitudes such as "We want values like the 1950s and prosperity like the 1980s." Now, those things are all well and good, but what do they have to do with me? I wasn't alive in the 1950s to see what the values of America were, and I wasn't around in the 1980s to see the booming economy. Again, it is good to bring those examples up as points when you are trying to change minds on America's future, but they are wholly unconvincing when trying to get someone excited about conservatism, espe-cially young people. I'm a 25-year-old guy, and I never experienced any of those times, so referencing them has no real relevance to my life or what I want my future to be like. The left, instead of looking to the past of what they want our country to be like, looks to the future and has a hard, concrete plan. They say things such as "In 10 years, we want to defund the police. By 2030 we want no more fossil fuels. If I get elected, I will make college free." Although their ideas are bad, you can't deny the fact that they have a solid, succinct plan, and this is why conservatives lose. Young people in America right now hear the left's plan that is tangible and something they can actually look forward to and are incredibly attracted to it. They like that much more than just hearing the defense from conservatives: "We want the police, we don't want to end fossil fuels, and we don't want free college." If conservatives want to win the culture and win the hearts and minds of the next generation, the first thing we have to do is come up with a plan that people can actually tangibly get behind and support.

So, what do conservatives actually push forward as a plan for America? Well, one thing is absolutely the most important, cannot be sacrificed, and cannot be undermined: bringing God back to America or, what I say in my speeches: let's make God great again. It is more important now than ever for conservatives to make this not just a part but the forefront of our plan, by bringing Judeo-Christian values back to America. One of the most important lessons from the Bible that Dennis Prager ever taught me was about the first two verses of the Bible. Genesis 1:1 says, "In the beginning God created the heavens and the earth," which shows his immeasurable and perfect power. Genesis 1:2 then goes on to say, "Now the earth was formless and empty, darkness was over the surface of the deep, and the Spirit of God was hovering over the waters." God created the universe, and in this formless emptiness God created everything and God created order.

Without God, there can be no order, only chaos, and the left thrives on chaos. Thinking men can menstruate is chaos. Socialism is chaos. Calling everyone a racist who disagrees with them is chaos. The left has replaced God with their religion of leftism, and thus everything they touch turns to chaos. Without an obedience to God, America will fall to the left's chaos. But it is not just an obedience; it is an evangelical approach to God. In all of our lives, we must be disciples for Him and relay His message all across America. We have to share it in our communities, with our families and friends, and everywhere we see. I'll be honest; you will probably be called a "Bible-thumping conservative," but just as we see in Scripture in Romans 6:23, "For the wages of sin is death, but the free gift of God is eternal life in Christ Jesus our Lord." You will find true bliss and comfort in Him, not in what you find on this earth, and the judgments of others should not cause you to stray from God. It is imperative that every person in America realizes this fact, and it is up to all of us to try to make this happen. I've always said that if every person in the world followed the Ten Commandments, the world would be a better place, and you would be hard-pressed to find any atheist who would disagree with that fact. The values and truth within the Bible are what will bring America back from the chaos we see our country in, and bringing those values back has to be our first and most important priority.

One of the most important things we have to remember is that no matter what happens in elections, in this country, or in anything else, God is in control. This fact is easy to forget or miss. It is easy for me even in my day-to-day life to see all the horrible things going on in California and in this country and think how hopeless everything is. But at the end of the day, I always know God has a plan, and He's got this. People nowadays put far too much faith in their political leaders when they should be putting it in God. And even if they don't put it in God for whatever reason, they should at least be putting it in their families and values, not in elections and material objects. As we have lost God in America, people have put their faith in government above God or put faith in selfishness over family, and this is why there has been such a breakdown.

Exodus 20:12 states as the Fifth Commandment, "Honor your father and mother. Then you will live a long, full life in the land the Lord your God is giving you." People put aside family and thus put aside God, and then we see a breakdown of our country. If people honored their parents as much as they honored the influencers they saw on Instagram or AOC, the world would be a much better place. I can't put all the blame on individuals, though; a lot of this blame has to go on parents. If parents taught their children from a young age good values and personal responsibility, then there wouldn't be such a breakdown in this country. I hear every single day from people on social media about how "I'm a hardcore conservative patriot, but my kids are total leftists who hate my ideas and values." Parents have to take more of a real interest in their kids' lives and get them on the right path early. Keep your kid from seeing horrible leftist thoughts on social media, have them talk to you about what they learn in school and explain to them the right things, and read them Scripture from the Bible. A strong family unit is the pinnacle of American society, and without it America will crumble.

When I was in high school and college, I never called my mom unless I needed something. My relationship with my family was poor, so I turned to debauchery and victimhood and leftism. Now as a newly baptized conservative Christian, I make sure to text my mom every day and call her every week to see how she is doing. I cannot stress to you enough how important it is that you put family at the forefront of your life structure. It will make you a happier, more stable person, and you will be a thousand times better off for reestablishing those family relationships and honoring your mother and father.

So, we have gone through the two most important things to focus on in a vision for America. The first is putting God at the forefront, and the second is having a strong family unit. These are more tangible for the individual, but that is why they are the most important. You have to fix yourself and your own surroundings before you can focus on the world around you and other people. As Jordan Peterson says, "Set your house in perfect order before you criticize the world." After you have done that, we can focus on the more outward plans for conservatives. The first thing conservatives should focus on is taking back the education system. Now, that sounds like a daunting and very large goal, but I have always liked big goals. Big goals with little goals inside them can give you measurable results for a bigger purpose. It is how I live my life, and it hasn't failed me yet. We have to fix the education system, and we have to do it fast. Ronald Reagan famously said, "Freedom is never more than one generation away from extinction. We didn't pass it to our children in the bloodstream." All of the values that I talked about before, a fear of God and an emphasis on family, should be taught in schools, not the garbage they are teaching children now.

The silver lining of the coronavirus pandemic and having kids home from school is that parents were able to see what their children were being taught, and many of them were completely shocked. Transgenderism and how there are more than two genders, critical race theory, adult and grotesque sexual education, and a rewriting of American history are being taught to children as early as elementary school, and this cannot be allowed to continue. It doesn't matter what Republicans do in Congress, what conservative social media influencers say on Twitter, or what right-wing news reports on. If all of America's youth continues to be indoctrinated, then they will be leftists as they grow up with what they learned in school. Many kids see their teachers more than they see their own parents, so it is imperative that conservatives come up with a plan to stop the brain-washing we see in our schools. The teachers' unions need to lose power, school choice needs to be enacted nationwide, and curriculums need to be given a standard that takes away the teacher's ability to put fierce leftist political bias within them. Elected officials, along with everyday conservative Americans, need to push for this to become a reality and make sure children across this country are being educated in the right way.

When you stop having the Pledge of Allegiance recited in schools and replace it with teachings from Black Lives Matter, you know you have a big problem. When I was in college after Trump won in 2016, I remember that the day after the election some of my classes were canceled essentially for a "mourning day," and students gathered in the outside quad holding hands and crying instead of going to class. This cannot be the America our youth is brought up in, and kids need to be taught good values at their schools.

Unbiased civics education also needs to be at the forefront. When I interview students on basic civics questions on campuses, I am just completely floored by the lack of knowledge and understanding they have of American history. They don't know who the first president was, they don't know the three branches of government, and they don't even know who the vice president

is. But they can for sure tell you that this country is racist, climate change is destroying us, and police brutality
is the worst problem in America. In order to make a
change, good values have to be taught in schools in conjunction with what parents are teaching their kids, and
it has to be done in every generation with every child in
this country. If we don't take back education from the
left, everything we fight for every day means nothing
because the next generation of kids will be just as brainwashed as the last and then the next generation and the
next after that. We have to make solid, real changes in
our education system that will last for generations so
that we no longer have to fear the indoctrination being
put forth on our children.

After we focus on education, next comes opportunity. Remember before how I was talking about the left's
promises and their vision that give young people a real
plan to latch onto? Part of this is because young people
are lazy and entitled and free stuff sounds great, but a
lot of it is due to opportunity. The old school Republican
message is "Pick yourself up by your bootstraps," and
although there is still a lot of truth to that in America, the American dream is vanishing fast for people in
my generation. Imagine being a 20-something-year-old
fresh out of college with $100,000 in student debt and a
degree that thousands of other people also got, with no

real experience or skills. The price of education has gone up, the price of healthcare has gone up, and the price of rent and housing has gone up, and are all continuing to rise as the government and cronyism get heavily involved in all of those sectors. At this point, what are you supposed to do with your life? You see the left's plan to give you free things, you're attracted to it, and you feel like you don't need to work so hard because the government will take care of everything. But at the same time you think the government is "taking care of you," you're actually slipping deeper into debt.

Millennials today carry 16 percent of the nation's liabilities, which is disproportionately high. Maybe you end up getting a job, but your real (adjusted-for-inflation) wages end up being lower than the wages of past generations (Gen Xers and baby boomers) at the same age. Millennials today only own 3 percent of the nation's wealth, whereas baby boomers at the same age owned 21 percent of the nation's wealth, a stark difference. Millennials today are poorer, less happy, less responsible, and less stable than any generation we have seen in recent American history. We see as well when millennials have lower incomes and less wealth, they are slower to start families and buy houses, two benchmarks of a responsible adult. Millennials remain in apartments or at their parents' place and single for longer, making it even harder to become real adults and be financially stable. Also, without starting a family, as we talked about earlier, millennials are missing out on important values, lessons, and responsibilities they need for a happy, productive life. This is creating a stalled life for an entire generation, and the next generation (Gen Z) may have it even worse.

Now, back to the whole "picking yourself up by your bootstraps" argument from before. I want to reiterate: it is not impossible in the slightest to work hard and make something of yourself in America. I dropped out of college and am a perfect example of that mentality. But not everyone has the skills or passion that I have for what I wanted to do. Also, with full humility, what I do is incredibly difficult to succeed in. The majority of youth, when interviewed, choose "YouTube influencer" as a dream career, like they may have chosen "rock star" or "athlete" or "astronaut" in the past. Ninety-nine percent will never have the talent to be an influencer/speaker (or athlete or famous musician). Of the 1 percent who have talent, few will ever be able to crack through regardless.

Some people just want to make a living and provide for themselves, and that is a perfectly fine life to live. Let's imagine again you are that same millennial college graduate from the previous paragraph and you have decided you want to start your own business. Let's say you want to start a little T-shirt company. You set it up in your apartment and build your own website, and now you are ready to start selling. But it turns out you have to package all the shirts in your living room and buy all the materials for shipping and postage and run the website and keep up with the growing demand of online shopping. Then you see Amazon selling the same type of shirt as you from China for a fraction of the price, pushing you out and making it nearly impossible for you to make a profit. Or maybe you want to start a carpentry business. But then as soon as you want to start your own shop, a huge home repair conglomerate opens up in your town that hires cheap labor and gets its products from China and lobbies the government for special privileges, making your little carpentry business obsolete. Do you see what I am getting at here? America has become so corporatized with huge multibillion-dollar companies that starting a new small business is nearly impossible. Then these massive corporations lobby the government for regulations that snuff out small businesses and competition, and you have a recipe for disaster. You can't compete with these giants, and the small business American dream dies. This isn't a "free market"; this is cronyism and monopolies. Decades ago, a college grad could start a local brick-and-mortar business with hustle and guidance; today regulations and cost structures make doing so almost impossible.

Of course, there are still possibilities for innovation and new companies in the market now—I don't want to make it seem like there is no shot for people at all—but the compliance costs and regulations and big business destroying competition make it much more difficult than it ever was for your parents or your parents' parents. And the big corporations get away with this because they pay off politicians, giving them money in exchange for special privileges. What the politicians call "donations," I call bribery, and that is all it is. Until we hold politicians and businesses accountable for their treachery, we will continue to see a decline in the wealth owned by generations to come, and instead that wealth will be in the pockets of CEOs like Jeff Bezos.

I understand fully that many staunch libertarian, free-market capitalist types won't like my message here and think that an unregulated free market will just "work itself out." But what you have to understand about this is that it is not capitalism. It is big business taking advantage of the little guy. If you really believe in a free-market economy with competition where businesses rise and fall, then the first step to doing that is letting small businesses have a chance in this country. I mean, let's just look at what happened during this pandemic and the lockdowns. According to Yelp data, 60 percent of businesses that closed are going to remain closed permanently, a total of about 98,000 businesses as of September 2020. On the other hand, in Amazon's last quarter in October 2020, the business tripled its profits from the same quarter the year before. Big business stores never had to shut their doors or stop operations, while small businesses across the country were forced to close down. How come during the lockdown I could walk into a Macy's and get something from there, but the small furniture store down the street had to shut down? Are you starting to see how this was all coordinated? Big businesses that could pay off politicians very likely did for special privileges, while small businesses suffered.

The most egregious of all of these is big pharma. A lot of people hear about big pharma and think, "That sounds bad" but have no idea why it's actually bad. We pay more for healthcare per capita than any other country because of big pharma lobbying. No other developed country has this problem like we do, and the masses of middlemen lobbying for big pharma/big healthcare (including insurers and hospitals) get paid millions every year.

In a country where conservatives think, "We can

just vote for Republicans and everything will get better," we saw both Republicans and Democrats bend over backward to give big pharma total immunity over vaccine-related injuries and deaths with the creation of the National Vaccine Injury Compensation Program, just as *one* example. What this means is that if something bad happens to you when you take a vaccine, you cannot sue the vaccine or drug company for damages. Big pharma paid off politicians on both sides of the aisle to make this happen, and now instead of paying people for when their medicines are faulty, they instead don't have to do any of that, and *you*, the taxpayer, are responsible for paying for these damages. This council is essentially a government program that uses tax dollars to pay people damages from faulty or damaging vaccines. They have paid out roughly $4 billion in damages to date, and because it is a government program that is basically a bureaucratic secret court nightmare, that number could really be much higher. But the bureaucracy is so bad it is incredibly difficult to get paid out from this program. If that isn't corporate socialism, I don't know what it is. Big pharma continues to make billions upon billions of dollars while the taxpayers are responsible for paying for their problems.

Imagine if your family and a hundred other people ate at a burger joint and then every person who ate a burger ended up dead. You could sue the burger company. Or imagine 10 airplanes fell apart in the air and killed people. You could sue the airplane manufacturer for damages. With big pharma you can't sue them for damages, and if you need money for the damages that happened to you, the taxpayer is responsible for paying you as the company that hurt you makes money hand over fist laughing on its way to the bank. And this is only one example of big pharma's lobbying. When people talk about the swamp, this is exactly what they mean. As another example, what punishment have you seen from the self-created opioid crisis pharma unleashed on the country?

This type of scenario isn't unique to big pharma. This happens with big tech, big defense, and plenty of other million-dollar corporations around America. So, how do we fix this, and how does this tie into a conservative vision for America? If we want young people to have opportunities in America and take back control of our economy, conservatives need to push for a public option for campaign financing and cut the lobbyists out. This is another controversial take—I know, Bernie Sanders endorsed a public option—but I can guarantee you it is exactly what we need. This is how we get the cronyism and corporate socialism out of politics. There is more unity in left-wing and right-wing populism than there is in conservatism and leftism. It's also why so many Sanders supporters moved over to Trump instead of voting for Clinton in 2016.

What is a public option? With a public option, political candidates essentially get their campaign funding from the government, not from all these hidden dark money super political action committee (PAC) donations and special interests. Let's say I'm running for governor of California as a Republican, and there is one opponent who is a Democrat. The government allots us, let's say, $500,000 each, and that is the total money we are allowed to spend for our campaign. This means politicians can't get special donations from big pharma or from another corporate interest to snuff out opponents and sell our country out. We have to get rid of PACs and have donations be public record. Even if a donation is made to a politician, this would be public record, and couldn't be used for their campaign since it is outside the allotted public option money, and should not be tax deductible.

All these things won't completely fix the mess we have in the swamp in Washington, D.C., and around the country—people will always try to find ways to abuse the system—but this will help make it so that our politicians are public servants again and aren't just making millions of dollars hand over fist as they sell us out. Again, using Republicans as an example, in 2016, Republicans had control of the House, Senate, and presidency, and they couldn't even defund Planned Parenthood. Forget trying to outlaw abortion; they couldn't even get Planned Parenthood defunded!

Our vision for America is not just "electing Republicans" and hoping that fixes all our problems. Some of the loudest voices against big tech openly take most of their campaign funding from big tech, so there is a lot of "talk" but never any "action." The masses sit there eagerly reading every word in the articles when threats are thrown about, while the same fake politicians say, "We're going to get to the bottom of this" again and again.

Our conservative vision for America would guarantee that all politicians can't sell us out and are forced to follow through on the promises they make on the campaign trail and unable to be bought off by special interests. Then we can start to elect people who actually share our values and want to see some good done in this country, not just people who make false promises and are getting into politics to make their millions of dollars.

Imposing term limits is also thrown about as a solution, but the biggest problem is the people who can make this happen would be imposing term limits on themselves, and they never seem eager to give up their power.

The last thing to focus on for our conservative vision for America is culture. Culture in America now is completely centralized. Think about where you and most people you know get their news: Apple News, CNN, big social media sites. The days of your small-town *Cheyenne (Wyoming) Post* local newspaper are over, and everyone gets their news and information from their phone. There are no local community values being driven into people from small-town news and local communities; it is all manufactured in San Francisco, Los Angeles, and New York, where all the big tech, media, and advertising companies are located.

Think about advertising as an example as well. A car company, for example, would make ads tailored to specific groups and locations, like a city truck for people in a metro area or a family vehicle for a midwestern couple. It had targeted marketing, using everything from food props to actor ethnicities to match the markets where the TV ads were being shown. Nowadays, car companies just put leftism in all their ads, like virtue signaling to BLM in a commercial for potato chips. Like, what the hell does Black Lives Matter have to do with a tasty salty snack? Those same people in that small town who used to read their daily local newspaper now gets all their news from CNN and the *Washington Post* while watching ads on TV and on their phone that go completely against their values. Their new values are now created by some blue-haired UC Berkeley grad at an ad agency in New York instead of by their church, their parents, or their friends. The new values that have been created for us by the leftist media machine are all artificial and are the new standard for values in this country. Instead of familial, God-centered, community values, we have national, corporate, leftist values with little to no room for any dissidence. Leftist culture is inescapable, and it is driving America into a brainwashed country where up is down and bad is good.

Our final step for a conservative vision for America is decentralizing culture. We have to take the power away from big tech and big media companies who infiltrate our brains with nonsense constantly and bring good values back to the forefront of culture. This could be having more conservatives fighting to get into media firms. This means turning off CNN and doing your own research away from the ease of just opening Twitter and seeing the latest national leftist headline. This means being strong in your values when you see leftist culture taking hold around you. Don't be subservient to how they want you to act and feel; be courageous in your convictions, and speak up when you see evil, misguided things happen around you. This means doing the mass boycott movements the left does when a corporation starts virtue signaling leftism and pounding it with phone calls and letters to show it that at least half the country does not approve.

That is my conservative vision for America. I could really write a whole book about what our vision for America should be, but alas it is relegated to this final chapter. I know it is easy in our everyday lives to hear this vision and hear what we should really be doing and be afraid. It is much easier to walk a path of ignorance, not think about these things, and say, "Someone else will handle it." But I say the reason we are in the position we are in now is because of statements like that. Instead of standing up for ourselves, our values, or our communities, we have capitulated to the left and let them run America however they see fit. That time of cowering and ignorance has to be over for conservatives. The time to be brave is now, and although it is frightening, it is truly the only path we can take. As I have been able to talk to people and educate them and see their minds opened up and lives changed with just a few questions I ask, I have never felt more excited for the future of this country. If the people with whom I talk can have their minds changed, the same can be done for everyone you speak with. It's all about just having the courage to actually go and ask those questions. I know you can do it.

The number one thing you can do, with all of the information in this book and everything you believe in, is to never sacrifice your values for anything or anyone. All the information in this book that you just read means nothing if it just floats around in your head. This knowledge, these tactics, and these values must be used to spread good across America, or this book is meaningless.

Take what you have learned and what you believe in, and spread it to every single person you know at your church, on your campus, at your job, on social media, during family gatherings, on your dates, and when you meet anyone new. The key to saving America isn't just the best facts or a vision or a plan—it is you. You and everyone else who believes in what you do must go out and be proactive with their knowledge and values because the passive opposite will be the end of this country as we know it. And don't just stop with yourself. Convince others around you to speak up and stand up and have conversations, even when they're daunting or terrifying. J. R. R. Tolkien, the author of my favorite books, *The Lord of the Rings* series, once said, "It is not the strength of the body that counts, but the strength of the spirit." Be courageous, stand up to evil whenever you see it, and fight for what you know is right and good. It is better to stand and fail for what you believe in than to live on your knees.

Acknowledgments

· · · · · · · · · · · · · · · ·

So many people helped me make this book, and I am forever grateful to every single one of them.

First, I must show my gratitude to Dennis Prager. Dennis has been my mentor and friend and has taught me so much about politics, culture, faith, and how to live life. He has also been my guide while working at PragerU, showing me how to grow into the position where I am now. Without his advice and lessons for me, I never would be at the place I am now.

I also have to give a big thanks to everyone at Hachette/Center Street. Katie, Sean, Daisy, Eliot, Patsy, Alex, and Rudy have all been incredibly helpful, and for my first time writing a book having no idea what I was doing, they all helped me constantly and were there for me whenever I needed it.

ACKNOWLEDGMENTS

Everyone at the Fedd Agency has also been so helpful in this process, and Esther, Danielle, and Kyle worked incredibly hard with me to make this whole thing a success. I also have to give a shout-out to Esther specifically, who took a chance on me with this book and helped me get all of this started.

I must give a special thanks to Craig Strazzeri. Craig has been my biggest supporter at PragerU and has taught me everything I know about marketing, social media, and growing my audience. Craig has always been in my corner and has always supported my ambition and whatever ridiculous ideas I came to him with. Despite driving a feminine car, Craig has been an incredible role model for me and is someone who I really look up to and always go to if I ever need help.

All of the staff at PragerU, specifically our CEO Marissa Streit, and our CFO Layne Thrasher, has been so supportive during this whole process, and has given me incredible advice and guidance along the way.

Alex Guerra has been my best friend for years now, and without him in Los Angeles with me surrounded by all the leftists, I don't know where I would be. He has supported and pushed me and been there for me through the hardest of times.

Thank you to Jake Buol, who was the one of the biggest helps in the creation of this book. Without his help with research and support, this project never would have been possible.

I have to thank Pastor Jack Hibbs, who baptized me and has been my guide through finding my faith.

Thank you to my stepdad Bob, who kept pushing me forward.

Thank you to my sister Maddy, who has always been my biggest fan and supporter, and although I haven't seen him in years, thank you to my brother Zach, who helped me grow up and taught me how to be a man.

Thank you to my grandma Cookie for always pushing me to learn and read. I must give a special shout-out to my grandpa Chocolate, who was my best friend growing up, and since I didn't have a father, he was my father. Thank you to Chocolate for teaching me what real masculinity is, and for guiding me on how to be a leader.

Lastly, I have to thank my mom. Thank you for teaching me discipline, hard work, and courage. My mom's guidance throughout my life has made me the man I am today, and despite all the hardships, struggles, and mistakes I made, she was always there to help me. I couldn't have done any of this without her, and she has been my most important person in not just writing this book, but life in general.

Resources

· · · · · · · · · · ·

Chapter 1: Racism

"Benjamin Franklin's Anti-Slavery Petitions to Congress." National
Archives and Records Administration. Accessed June 4, 2021.
www.archives.gov/legislative/features/franklin.

"Buffalo School District Mandates New York Times' 1619 Project in Curriculum." Young America's Foundation. March
6, 2020. Accessed June 4, 2021. www.yaf.org/news/buffalo
-school-district-mandates-new-york-times-1619-project-in
-curriculum/.

Bureau, US Census. "21.3% of US Population Participates in Government Assistance Programs Each Month." The United States
Census Bureau. May 28, 2015. Accessed June 4, 2021. www
.census.gov/newsroom/press-releases/2015/cb15-97.html.

Connor, Phillip, and Gustavo López. "5 Facts about the U.S.
Rank in Worldwide Migration." Pew Research Center. May
18, 2016. Accessed June 4, 2021. www.pewresearch.org/fact
-tank/2016/05/18/5-facts-about-the-u-s-rank-in-worldwide
-migration/.

"Finally, The Truth About Welfare—How Many Blacks Vs. How
Many Whites." Accessed June 4, 2021. www.lowincome.org

RESOURCES

/2016/04/truth-about-welfare-foodstamps-how-many-blacks
-vs-whites.html.

Fisher, Max. "A Fascinating Map of the World's Most and Least
Racially Tolerant Countries." The Washington Post. May 16,
2013. Accessed June 4, 2021. www.washingtonpost.com
/news/worldviews/wp/2013/05/15/a-fascinating-map-of-the
-worlds-most-and-least-racially-tolerant-countries/.

Hennessy-Fiske, Molly. " 'We Don't Have Law and Order': Black
and Latino Business Owners Face Destruction in Minneapolis."
Los Angeles Times. May 29, 2020. Accessed June 4, 2021. www
.latimes.com/world-nation/story/2020-05-29/minneapolis
-minority-business-owners-awake-to-destruction.

"Marriage and Divorce: Patterns by Gender, Race, and Educa-
tional Attainment." Monthly Labor Review. U.S. Bureau
of Labor Statistics. October 1, 2013. Accessed June 4, 2021.
www.bls.gov/opub/mlr/2013/article/marriage-and-divorce
-patterns-by-gender-race-and-educational-attainment.htm.

Mobilewalla. "New Report Reveals Demographics of Black
Lives Matter Protesters Shows Vast Majority Are White,
Marched Within Their Own Cities." PR Newswire. June 18,
2020. Accessed June 4, 2021. www.prnewswire.com/news
-releases/new-report-reveals-demographics-of-black-lives
-matter-protesters-shows-vast-majority-are-white-marched
-within-their-own-cities-301079234.html.

Parker, Wayne. "Statistics on Fatherless Children in America."
LiveAbout. May 24, 2019. Accessed June 4, 2021. www.live-
about.com/fatherless-children-in-america-statistics-1270392.

"Slavery and the Abolition Society." Benjamin Franklin Historical Society. Accessed June 4, 2021. www.benjamin-franklin
-history.org/slavery-abolition-society/.

Stockman, Farah. " 'She Was Part of This Family': Jefferson
Descendants Reflect on Sally Hemings Exhibit." The New
York Times. June 16, 2018. Accessed June 4, 2021. www

.nytimes.com/2018/06/16/us/jefferson-sally-hemings
-descendants.html.

Thernstrom, Abigail, and Stephan Thernstrom. "Black Progress:
How Far We've Come, and How Far We Have to Go." Brookings. March 1, 1998. Accessed June 4, 2021. www.brookings
.edu/articles/black-progress-how-far-weve-come-and-how
-far-we-have-to-go/.

Washington, Jesse. "Blacks Struggle with 72 Percent Unwed Mothers Rate." NBC News. November 7, 2010. Accessed June 4, 2021.
www.nbcnews.com/id/39993685/ns/health-womens_health/t
/blacks-struggle-percent-unwed-mothers-rate/#.X4JhnS2z1ZJ.

Wilcox, W. Bradford, Robert I. Lerman, and Joseph Price.
"Mobility and Money in U.S. States: The Marriage Effect."
Brookings. December 7, 2015. Accessed June 4, 2021. www
.brookings.edu/research/mobility-and-money-in-u-s-states
-the-marriage-effect/.

Wineburg, Sam. "Undue Certainty." American Federation
of Teachers. 2012. Accessed June 23, 2021. https://www
.aft.org/periodical/american-educator/winter-2012-2013
/undue-certainty.

Chapter 2: Coronavirus

Barke, Jeffrey I. *COVID-19: A Physicians Take on the Exaggerated Fear
of the Coronavirus*. S.l.: Americas Group Publications, 2021.

"COVID-19 in Primary Schools: No Significant Transmission
among Children or from Students to Teachers." Institut Pasteur. June 23, 2020. Accessed June 4, 2021. www.pasteur.fr
/en/press-area/press-documents/covid-19-primary-schools-no
-significant-transmission-among-children-students-teachers.

"COVID-19 Provisional Counts—Weekly Updates by Select
Demographic and Geographic Characteristics." Centers for
Disease Control and Prevention. May 26, 2021. Accessed

June 4, 2021. www.cdc.gov/nchs/nvss/vsrr/covid_weekly/index.htm.

Derwand, Roland, Martin Scholz, and Vladimir Zelenko. "COVID-19 Outpatients: Early Risk-stratified Treatment with Zinc plus Low-dose Hydroxychloroquine and Azithromycin: A Retrospective Case Series Study." International Journal of Antimicrobial Agents. December 2020. Accessed June 4, 2021. www.ncbi.nlm.nih.gov/pmc/articles/PMC7587171/.

Dougherty, Jon. "Newsom's Winery Remains Open While Other California Wineries Ordered to Shut Down Over COVID." BizPac Review. December 20, 2020. Accessed June 4, 2021. www.bizpacreview.com/2020/12/20/newsoms-winery-remains-open-while-other-california-wineries-ordered-to-shut-down-over-covid-1007890/.

"German Study Shows Low Coronavirus Infection Rate in Schools." U.S. News & World Report. July 13, 2020. Accessed June 4, 2021. www.usnews.com/news/world/articles/2020-07-13/german-study-shows-low-coronavirus-infection-rate-in-schools.

Huber, Colleen. "Masks Are Neither Effective nor Safe: A Summary of the Science." Technocracy News. July 14, 2020. Accessed June 4, 2021. www.technocracy.news/masks-are-neither-effective-nor-safe-a-summary-of-the-science/?fbclid=IwAR3PVzISD7bZIZ4DF8cXANX2S6o-dBHdN8yyQpF-jNNxCcy3Q_F9MGL1UYw.

Jefferson, T., M.A. Jones, L. Al-Ansary, G.A. Bawazeer, E.M. Beller, J. Clark, J.M. Conly, C. Del Mar, E. Dooley, E. Ferroni, P. Glasziou, T. Hoffmann, S. Thorning, and M.L. van Driel. "Physical Interventions to Interrupt or Reduce the Spread of Respiratory Viruses. Part 1—Face Masks, Eye Protection and Person Distancing: Systematic Review and Meta-analysis." MedRxiv. April 7, 2020. Accessed June 4, 2021. www.medrxiv.org/content/10.1101/2020.03.30.20047217v2.

RESOURCES

Kim, Soo. "Florida Man Killed in Crash Listed as COVID-19 Death, Raising Doubts over Health Data." Newsweek. July 20, 2020. Accessed June 4, 2021. www.newsweek.com/florida -man-killed-crash-listed-covid-19-death-raising-doubts-over -health-data-1518994.

Klompas, Michael, et al., Author Affiliations from the Department of Population Medicine, R.W. Frenck and Others, F.P. Polack and Others, and T.T. Shimabukuro and Others. "Universal Masking in Hospitals in the Covid-19 Era." The New England Journal of Medicine. May 21, 2020. Accessed June 4, 2021. www.nejm.org/doi/full/10.1056/nejmp2006372.

Ladapo, Joseph A. "Opinion | Too Much Caution Is Killing Covid Patients." The Wall Street Journal. November 24, 2020. Accessed June 4, 2021. www.wsj.com/articles/too-much -caution-is-killing-covid-patients-11606238928.

Lewis, Dyani. "Why Schools Probably Aren't COVID Hotspots." Nature News. October 29, 2020. Accessed June 4, 2021. www .nature.com/articles/d41586-020-02973-3.

Luna, Taryn. "Photos Raise Doubts about Newsom's Claim that Dinner with Lobbyist was Outdoors amid COVID-19 Surge" Los Angeles Times. November 18, 2020. Accessed June 4, 2021. www.latimes.com/california/story/2020-11-18/newsom -french-laundry-dinner-explanation-photos-jason-kinney -california-medical-association-covid-19.

Mehra, Mandeep. "Retraction—Hydroxychloroquine or chloroquine with or without a macrolide for treatment of covid-19: a multinational registry analysis." The Lancet. June 5, 2020. Accessed June 24, 2021. https://www.thelancet.com /journals/lancet/article/PIIS0140-6736(20)31324-6/fulltext.

"Scientists Find No Significant COVID-19 Transmission among Children or from Students to Teachers in Primary Schools." Healthcare Purchasing News. June 25, 2020. Accessed June 4, 2021. www.hpnonline.com/infection-prevention/screening

-surveillance/article/21143692/scientists-find-no-significant
-covid19-transmission-among-children-or-from-students-to
-teachers-in-primary-schools.

Chapter 3: Freedom of Speech

"ACLU History: Taking a Stand for Free Speech in Skokie." American Civil Liberties Union. September 1, 2010. Accessed June 5, 2021. www.aclu.org/other/aclu-history-taking-stand-free-speech-skokie.

Bischoff, Paul. "Internet Censorship 2021: A Global Map of Internet Restrictions." Comparitech. January 15, 2020. Accessed June 5, 2021. www.comparitech.com/blog/vpn-privacy/internet-censorship-map/.

Emmons, Libby. "BREAKING: New York Post Locked out of Twitter after Publishing Biden Bombshell." The Post Millennial. October 15, 2020. Accessed June 5, 2021. thepostmillennial.com/breaking-ny-post-locked-out-of-twitter.

"Nazi Propoganda and Censorship." United States Holocaust Memorial Museum. January 15, 2021. Accessed June 5, 2021. encyclopedia.ushmm.org/content/en/article/nazi-propaganda-and-censorship.

"PragerU Takes Legal Action Against Google and YouTube for Discrimination." PragerU. Accessed June 5, 2021. www.prageru.com/press-release/prageru-takes-legal-action-against-google-and-youtube-for-discrimination/.

"Why is Freedom of Speech So Unique in the United States? (Excerpt)." Carnegie Council for Ethics in International Affairs. Accessed June 5, 2021. www.carnegiecouncil.org/education/worksheets/ushistory/usgovt/speech.

"World Report 2019: Rights Trends in China." Human Rights Watch. January 17, 2019. Accessed June 5, 2021. www.hrw.org/world-report/2019/country-chapters/china-and-tibet#.

Chapter 4: Guns and the Second Amendment

"53 Shot, 5 Fatally, in Chicago Weekend Gun Violence." Chicago Sun-Times. October 12, 2020. Accessed June 6, 2021. chicago.suntimes.com/crime/2020/10/12/21510454/chicago-weekend-shootings-gun-violence-october-9-12-2020.

Akbar, Arifa. "Mao's Great Leap Forward 'Killed 45 Million in Four Years'." The Independent. October 23, 2011. Accessed June 5, 2021. www.independent.co.uk/arts-entertainment/books/news/maos-great-leap-forward-killed-45-million-in-four-years-2081630.html.

"Crime and Guns: Insights into the Sources of Crime Guns, Their Use, Regional/International Variations, and More." Gun Facts. April 9, 2021. Accessed June 6, 2021. www.gunfacts.info/gun-policy-info/crime-and-guns/.

Curren, Jenna. "FBI Report: In 2019, More People were Killed by Hands, Fists, and Feet than Rifles." Law Enforcement Today. October 10, 2020. Accessed June 6, 2021. www.lawenforcementtoday.com/fbi-in-2019-more-people-were-killed-by-hands-fists-and-feet-than-rifles/.

"Defensive Gun Uses in the U.S." The Heritage Foundation. May 10, 2021. Accessed June 6, 2021. www.heritage.org/data-visualizations/firearms/defensive-gun-uses-in-the-us/.

French, David. "Study: The Vast Majority of Gun Crime Isn't Committed by Lawful Gun Owners." National Review. August 12, 2016. Accessed June 5, 2021. www.nationalreview.com/corner/study-vast-majority-gun-crime-isnt-committed-lawful-gun-owners/.

Gramlich, John. "What the Data says about Gun Deaths in the U.S." Pew Research Center. August 16, 2019. Accessed June 6, 2021. www.pewresearch.org/fact-tank/2019/08/16/what-the-data-says-about-gun-deaths-in-the-u-s/.

RESOURCES

"Guatemala." The Center for Justice and Accountability. Accessed June 5, 2021. cja.org/where-we-work/guatemala/.

Halbrook, Stephen P. "How the Nazis Used Gun Control." National Review. December 2, 2013. Accessed June 5, 2021. www.nationalreview.com/2013/12/how-nazis-used-gun-control-stephen-p-halbrook/.

Hertzbach, Joe. "Most Mass Shootings Happen in Gun Free Zones." Image. February 27, 2018. Accessed June 6, 2021. attorneysforfreedom.com/blognews/mass-shootings-happen-gun-free-zones.

"Khmer Rouge: Cambodia's Years of Brutality." BBC News. November 16, 2018. Accessed June 5, 2021. www.bbc.com/news/world-asia-pacific-10684399.

Kifner, John. "Armenian Genocide of 1915: An Overview." The New York Times. December 7, 2007. Accessed June 5, 2021. archive.nytimes.com/www.nytimes.com/ref/timestopics/topics_armeniangenocide.html?mcubz=1.

"Knife Crime: Fatal Stabbings at Highest Level since Records Began in 1946." BBC News. February 7, 2019. Accessed June 6, 2021. www.bbc.com/news/uk-47156957.

"Tracking Chicago Shooting Victims." Chicago Tribune. June 3, 2021. Accessed June 6, 2021. www.chicagotribune.com/data/ct-shooting-victims-map-charts-htmlstory.html.

"Venezuela's Maduro Launches Civilian Disarmament Plan." BBC News. September 22, 2014. Accessed June 5, 2021. www.bbc.com/news/world-latin-america-29308509.

Chapter 5: Illegal Immigration

"DHS Launches New Center for Countering Human Trafficking." ICE.gov. October 20, 2020. Accessed June 6, 2021. www.ice.gov/news/releases/dhs-launches-new-center-countering-human-trafficking#.

RESOURCES

Gramlich, John. "How Border Apprehensions, ICE Arrests and Deportations Have Changed under Trump." Pew Research Center. March 2, 2020. Accessed June 6, 2021. www.pew research.org/fact-tank/2020/03/02/how-border-apprehensions -ice-arrests-and-deportations-have-changed-under-trump/.

"Infographic: Fiscal Burden of Illegal Immigration on Californians." Federation for American Immigration Reform. Accessed June 6, 2021. www.fairus.org/issue/workforce -economy/infographic-fiscal-burden-illegal-immigration -californians.

Raul. "This Chart Shows the Rising Cost of Border Security in the U.S." HowMuch. July 16, 2019. Accessed June 6, 2021. https://howmuch.net/sources/the-cost-of-border-security -and-immigration-enforcement-in-the-us.

Reynolds, Gerald A. "The Impact of Illegal Immigration on the Wages and Employment Opportunities of Black Workers." January 15, 2010. Accessed June 4, 2021. https://www.usccr .gov/pubs/docs/IllegImmig_10-14-10_430pm.pdf.

Sadler, Kelly. "The Real Cost of Illegal Immigration, and It's Not Avocados." The Washington Times. June 5, 2019. Accessed June 6, 2021. www.washingtontimes.com/news/2019/jun/5 /the-real-cost-of-illegal-immigration-and-its-not-a/.

Yack, Austin. "U.S. Taxpayers Pay about $1.2 Billion to Incarcerate Illegal Immigrants." National Review. May 2, 2017. Accessed June 6, 2021. www.nationalreview.com/corner/federal-prison -illegal-immigrants-taxpayers-pay-about-billion/.

Chapter 6: Family Values

Anderson, Jane. "The Impact of Family Structure on the Health of Children: Effects of Divorce." The Linacre Quarterly. November 2014. Accessed June 6, 2021. www.ncbi.nlm.nih .gov/pmc/articles/PMC4240051/.

RESOURCES

Battersby, Lucy. "The Survey Says ... Women Are Less Happy with Their Relationships than Men Are." The Sydney Morning Herald. July 15, 2015. Accessed June 6, 2021. www.smh.com.au/national/the-survey-says--women-are-less-happy-with-their-relationships-than-men-are-20150714-gibxpj.html.

Bhatia, Jahnavi. "BHATIA: Sweden Hasn't Achieved Gender Equality." The Daily Free Press. February 23, 2017. Accessed June 6, 2021. dailyfreepress.com/2017/02/23/bhatia-sweden-hasnt-achieved-gender-equality/.

Caruso, Catherine. "Men with Happier Childhoods Have Stronger Relationships in Old Age." Scientific American. October 19, 2016. Accessed June 6, 2021. www.scientificamerican.com/article/men-with-happier-childhoods-have-stronger-relationships-in-old-age/.

Fagan, Patrick. "The Real Root Causes of Violent Crime: The Breakdown of Marriage, Family, and Community." The Heritage Foundation. March 17, 1995. Accessed June 6, 2021. www.heritage.org/crime-and-justice/report/the-real-root-causes-violent-crime-the-breakdown-marriage-family-and#.

Galvin, Gaby. "Who Suicide Hits Hardest in the U.S." U.S. News & World Report. June 20, 2019. Accessed June 6, 2021. www.usnews.com/news/healthiest-communities/articles/2019-06-20/suicide-by-race-age-in-the-us.

Galvin, Gaby. "U.S. Marriage Rate Hits Historic Low." U.S. News & World Report. April 29, 2020. Accessed June 6, 2021. www.usnews.com/news/healthiest-communities/articles/2020-04-29/us-marriage-rate-drops-to-record-low.

Heid, Markham. "Why Do Women Live Longer Than Men?" Time. February 27, 2019. Accessed June 6, 2021. time.com/5538099/why-do-women-live-longer-than-men/.

Jeffreys, Branwen. "Do Children in Two-parent Families Do Better?" BBC News. February 5, 2019. Accessed June 6, 2021. www.bbc.com/news/education-47057787.

RESOURCES

"Why Have Divorce Rates Increased Over Time?" Attorneys
.com. Accessed June 6, 2021. www.attorneys.com/divorce
/why-have-divorce-rates-increased-over-time.

Chapter 7: Abortion

Hazlett, Courtney. "Justin Bieber's mom tells why she chose not to
abort at 17." Today. September 4, 2012. Accessed June 24, 2021.
https://www.today.com/news/justin-biebers-mom-tells-why
-she-chose-not-abort-17-999256.

"Prenatal Development and Types of Abortion." Live Action.
Accessed June 6, 2021. www.liveaction.org/learn/the-problem
/prenatal-development-abortion/.

"Seven Famous People Who Were Almost Aborted." LifeNews
.com. May 29, 2014. Accessed June 6, 2021. www.lifenews
.com/2014/05/29/seven-famous-people-who-were-almost
-aborted/.

Smith, Kate. "Abortion at 'Historic Low' by All Measures, New CDC
Study Says." CBS News. November 27, 2019. Accessed June
6, 2021. www.cbsnews.com/news/us-abortion-rate-number
-of-abortions-in-us-hits-historic-low-per-centers-for-disease
-control-study-today-2019-11-27/.

Warta, Tamara. "27 Famous Preemies." LoveToKnow. Accessed
June 6, 2021. baby.lovetoknow.com/wiki/Famous_Preemies.

Chapter 8: Police Brutality

Ehrenfreund, Max and Jeff Guo. "How a Controversial Study
Found That Police are More Likely to Shoot Whites, Not
Blacks." The Washington Post. July 13, 2016. Accessed June
7, 2021. www.washingtonpost.com/news/wonk/wp/2016
/07/13/why-a-massive-new-study-on-police-shootings-of
-whites-and-blacks-is-so-controversial/.

RESOURCES

Elder, Larry. "The Ferguson Lie." PragerU. June 22, 2020. Accessed June 7, 2021. www.prageru.com/video/the-ferguson-lie/.

Fox, Justin. "How Dangerous Is Police Work?" Bloomberg.com. June 23, 2020. Accessed June 7, 2021. www.bloomberg.com /opinion/articles/2020-06-23/how-dangerous-is-police-work.

Lehman, Charles Fain. "More Cops Means Less Crime, Analysis Shows." The Washington Free Beacon. February 14, 2018. Accessed June 7, 2021. freebeacon.com/issues/cops-means -less-crime-analysis-shows/.

Mac Donald, Heather. "There Is No Epidemic of Fatal Police Shoot-ings against Unarmed Black Americans." Manhattan Institute. September 3, 2020. Accessed June 7, 2021. www.manhattan -institute.org/police-black-killings-homicide-rates-race -injustice.

Moore, Tina, Larry Celona, and Amanda Woods. "Shootings Surge in NYC amid Disbanding of NYPD's Plainclothes Anti -crime Unit." New York Post. June 19, 2020. Accessed June 7, 2021. nypost.com/2020/06/19/nyc-shootings-surge-after -nypds-anti-crime-unit-disbanded/.

"People Shot to Death by U.S. Police, by Race 2017–2021." Statista. June 1, 2021. Accessed June 7, 2021. www.statista.com /statistics/585152/people-shot-to-death-by-us-police-by-race/.

Pollak, Joel B. "Fact Check: Police Do Kill More White People, but There's More to the Story." Breitbart. July 14, 2020. Accessed June 7, 2021. www.breitbart.com/crime/2020/07 /14/fact-check-police-do-kill-more-white-people-but-theres -more-to-the-story/.

Rambaran, Vandana. " 'Defund the Police' Movement Takes Toll on NYC's Crime Rate, Law Enforcement and Dem Critics Claim, as Shootings and Murders Spike." Fox News. October 8, 2020. Accessed June 7, 2021. www.foxnews.com/politics /nyc-defund-the-police-critics.

RESOURCES

Chapter 9: Cultural Appropriation

"Cultural Appropriation." Oxford Reference. Accessed June 7, 2021. www.oxfordreference.com/view/10.1093/oi/authority .20110803095652789.

Feeney, Nolan. "Katy Perry's 'Geisha-Style' Performance Needs to Be Called Out." The Atlantic. November 25, 2013. Accessed June 7, 2021. www.theatlantic.com/entertainment/archive /2013/11/katy-perrys-geisha-style-performance-needs-to-be -called-out/281805/.

McFeeters, Stephanie. "Counter-protesters Join Kimono Fray at MFA—The Boston Globe." BostonGlobe.com. July 18, 2015. Accessed June 7, 2021. www.bostonglobe.com/arts/2015/07 /18/counter-protesters-join-kimono-fray-mfa/ZgVWiT3y IZSlQgxCghAOFM/story.html.

Witt, Will. "Students Vs. Mexicans: Cultural Appropriation." PragerU. October 24, 2018. Accessed June 7, 2021. www .prageru.com/video/students-vs-mexicans-cultural-appro priation/.

Chapter 10: Cancel Culture

Day, Nate. "'Live PD' Production Ceased at A&E amid Protests, Civil Unrest." Fox News. June 10, 2020. Accessed June 7, 2021. www.foxnews.com/entertainment/live-pd-canceled -ae-protests-civil-unrest.

Chapter 11: Climate Change

"10 Beautiful Beachfront Estates Celebs Call Home." Domino. October 11, 2018. Accessed June 24, 2017. www.domino.com /content/celebrity-homes-beach/.

RESOURCES

"5 Fast Facts about Spent Nuclear Fuel." Energy.gov. March 30, 2020. Accessed June 7, 2021. www.energy.gov/ne/articles/5 -fast-facts-about-spent-nuclear-fuel.

Barnard, Michael. "How Many Wind Turbines Would It Take to Power The US?" Forbes. December 18, 2019. Accessed June 7, 2021. www.forbes.com/sites/quora/2019/12/18/how -many-wind-turbines-would-it-take-to-power-the-us/?sh =5cb8a22a1d96.

Davidson, John Daniel. "No, Polar Bears Are Not Dying off in Droves Because of Climate Change." The Federalist. January 5, 2018. Accessed June 7, 2021. thefederalist.com/2018/01 /05/no-polar-bears-not-dying-off-droves-climate-change/.

Hardy, Doug. "Greatest Snowfall on Kilimanjaro Glaciers in Years." GlacierHub. April 4, 2018. Accessed June 7, 2021. glacierhub.org/2018/04/04/greatest-snowfall-on-kilimanjaro -glaciers-in-years/.

J. Ken. "Amazing Map: Total Solar Panels to Power The United States." Modern Survival Blog. March 13, 2019. Accessed June 7, 2021. modernsurvivalblog.com/alternative-energy/amazing -total-area-of-solar-panels-to-power-the-united-states/.

Layne, Jordon. "Are Solar Panels Toxic or Bad for the Environment?" Ablison Energy. July 29, 2020. Accessed June 7, 2021. www.ablison.com/are-solar-panels-toxic-or-bad-for-the -environment/.

Lott, Maxim. "Top 5 Most Outrageous 2020 Doomsday Predictions That Didn't Pan Out." Fox News. January 1, 2020. Accessed June 7, 2021. www.foxnews.com/us/top-5-most -outrageous-2020-doomsday-predictions.

Marlo Lewis, Jr. "Climate-Related Deaths Are at Historic Lows, Data Show." FEE Freeman Article. June 7, 2019. Accessed June 7, 2021. fee.org/articles/climate-related-deaths-are-at -historic-lows-data-show/.

RESOURCES

"Nuclear Power is the Most Reliable Energy Source and It's Not Even Close." Energy.gov. March 24, 2021. Accessed June 7, 2021. www.energy.gov/ne/articles/nuclear-power-most-reliable-energy-source-and-its-not-even-close.

Shellenberger, Michael. "Why I Changed My Mind about Nuclear Power: Transcript of Michael Shellenberger's TEDx Berlin 2017." Environmental Progress. November 21, 2017. Accessed June 7, 2021. environmentalprogress.org/big-news/2017/11/21/why-i-changed-my-mind-about-nuclear-power-transcript-of-michael-shellenbergers-tedx-berlin-2017.

Shellenberger, Michael. "If Solar Panels Are So Clean, Why Do They Produce So Much Toxic Waste?" Forbes. May 23, 2018. Accessed June 7, 2021. www.forbes.com/sites/michaelshellenberger/2018/05/23/if-solar-panels-are-so-clean-why-do-they-produce-so-much-toxic-waste/?sh=71f4794f121c.

Themesberg. "Road to EU Climate Neutrality." EU Road to Climate Neutrality. Accessed June 7, 2021. www.roadtoclimateneutrality.eu/.

"U.S. Carbon (CO2) Emissions 1960–2021." MacroTrends. Accessed June 7, 2021. www.macrotrends.net/countries/USA/united-states/carbon-co2-emissions.

Chapter 12: Socialism

Carden, Art. "Yes, It Was 'Real Socialism.' No, We Shouldn't Try Again." Forbes. August 18, 2020. Accessed June 7, 2021. www.forbes.com/sites/artcarden/2020/08/18/yes-it-was-real-socialism-no-we-shouldnt-try-again/?sh=3b3ce9516260.

Dorfman, Jeffrey. "Sorry Bernie Bros but Nordic Countries Are Not Socialist." Forbes. July 8, 2018. Accessed June 7, 2021. www.forbes.com/sites/jeffreydorfman/2018/07/08/sorry-bernie-bros-but-nordic-countries-are-not-socialist/?sh=389eb52f74ad.

Hoffman, Susanna. "Socialism Didn't Work in Sweden, And It Won't Work in America." The Federalist. June 25, 2019. Accessed June 7, 2021. thefederalist.com/2019/06/25/socialism-didnt-work-in-sweden-and-it-wont-work-in-america/.

Norberg, Johan. "Sweden's Lessons for America." Cato.org. February 2020. Accessed June 7, 2021. www.cato.org/publications/policy-report/swedens-lessons-america.

"Timeline: Hugo Chavez's Rise to Power in Venezuela." CTVNews. March 5, 2013. Accessed June 7, 2021. www.ctvnews.ca/world/timeline-hugo-chavez-s-rise-to-power-in-venezuela-1.1182827.

Chapter 13: "Free" College

Easley, Jonathan. "Warren Confronted by Man at Campaign Event over Tuition Reimbursement." The Hill. January 23, 2020. Accessed June 7, 2021. thehill.com/homenews/campaign/479608-warren-confronted-by-man-at-campaign-event-over-tuition-reimbursement.

Friedman, Zack. "Student Loan Debt Statistics in 2020: A Record $1.6 Trillion." Forbes. February 3, 2020. Accessed June 7, 2021. www.forbes.com/sites/zackfriedman/2020/02/03/student-loan-debt-statistics/?sh=32140570281f.

Jamrisko, Michelle, and Ilan Kolet. "College Tuition Costs Soar: Chart of the Day." Bloomberg.com. August 18, 2014. Accessed June 7, 2021. www.bloomberg.com/news/articles/2014-08-18/college-tuition-costs-soar-chart-of-the-day.

Kirk, Charlie. "The Student Loan Bubble: A Crisis the Government Created." Townhall. April 27, 2013. Accessed June 7, 2021. townhall.com/columnists/charliekirk/2013/04/27/the-student-loan-bubble-a-crisis-the-government-created-n1579861.

Kirk, Charlie. "Game of Loans." PragerU. November 9, 2015. Accessed June 7, 2021. www.prageru.com/video/game-of-loans/.

"Rapidly Rising Student Debt Harms Low-Income Students."
U.S. News & World Report. January 4, 2012. Accessed June 7,
2021. www.usnews.com/education/blogs/student-loan-ranger
/2012/01/04/rapidly-rising-student-debt-harms-low-income
-students.

Sparshott, Jeffrey. "Congratulations, Class of 2015. You're the
Most Indebted Ever (For Now)." The Wall Street Journal.
May 8, 2015. Accessed June 7, 2021. blogs.wsj.com/economics
/2015/05/08/congratulations-class-of-2015-youre-the-most
-indebted-ever-for-now/.

Chapter 14: "Free" Healthcare

Chen, Lahnee, and Allen Estrin. "Why Is Health Insurance So
Complicated?" PragerU. September 4, 2017. Accessed June 7,
2021. www.prageru.com/video/why-is-health-insurance-so
-complicated/.

Chen, Lanhee, and Allen Estrin. "What's Wrong with Government-Run Healthcare?" PragerU. October 14, 2018. Accessed
June 7, 2021. www.prageru.com/video/whats-wrong-with
-government-run-healthcare/.

Kelly, Kel. "The Myth of Free-Market Healthcare." Mises Institute. March 9, 2011. Accessed June 7, 2021. mises.org/library
/myth-free-market-healthcare.

Landen, Rachel. "Pattern of Problems with Veterans Affairs
Healthcare System." Modern Healthcare. May 7, 2014.
Accessed June 7, 2021. www.modernhealthcare.com/article
/20140507/NEWS/305079939/pattern-of-problems-with
-veterans-affairs-healthcare-system.

Onge, Peter St. "Canadian Health Care: A Warning, Not a Beacon."
The Heritage Foundation. February 28, 2020. Accessed June
7, 2021. www.heritage.org/health-care-reform/commentary
/canadian-health-care-warning-not-beacon.

Onge, Peter St. "How Socialized Medicine Hurts Canadians and Leaves Them Worse Off Financially." The Heritage Foundation. February 20, 2020. Accessed June 7, 2021. www.heritage.org/health-care-reform/report/how-socialized-medicine-hurts-canadians-and-leaves-them-worse-financially.

Pipes, Sally C. "Canadians Pay a High Price for Free Health Care." Investor's Business Daily. August 14, 2018. Accessed June 7, 2021. www.investors.com/politics/columnists/canadians-high-price-health-care/.

Pipes, Sally C. "The Canadian Health-Care Scare." National Review. August 24, 2020. Accessed June 7, 2021. www.nationalreview.com/2020/08/canadian-single-payer-health-care-system-slow-inefficient/.

Schlapp, Mercedes. "Veterans Need Real Health Care Choices." U.S. News & World Report. May 26, 2014. Accessed June 7, 2021. www.usnews.com/opinion/mercedes-schlapp/2014/05/26/the-va-scandal-proves-government-needs-to-get-out-of-the-health-care-business.

"Single Payer and The Alfie Evans Nightmare Go Hand In Hand." Investor's Business Daily. April 30, 2018. Accessed June 7, 2021. www.investors.com/politics/editorials/alfie-evans-national-health-service-life-support-charlie-gard-socialized-medicine-single-payer/.

"3 Phoenix VA officials placed on leave amid scandal." Fox News. May 1, 2014. Accessed June 24, 2021.https://www.foxnews.com/politics/3-phoenix-va-officials-placed-on-leave-amid-scandal.

Chapter 15: Minimum Wage

"60 Million People Depend on the Incomes of Low-Wage Workers in America: Increasing the Federal Minimum Wage Would

RESOURCES

Benefit on Average More than 135,000 People in Each Congressional District." Economic Policy Institute. December 16, 2014. Accessed June 7, 2021. www.epi.org/press/60-million-people-depend-on-the-incomes-of-low-wage-workers-in-america-increasing-the-federal-minimum-wage-would-benefit-on-average-more-than-135000-people-in-each-congressional-district/.

Jardim, Ekaterina, Mark Long, Robert Plotnick, Emma Van Inwegen, Jacob Vigdor, and Hilary Wething. "Minimum Wage Increases, Wages, and Low-Wage Employment: Evidence from Seattle." *National Bureau of Economic Research*, 2017. doi:10.3386/w23532.

Kiger, Patrick J. "Minimum Wage in America: A Timeline." History.com. October 18, 2019. Accessed June 7, 2021. www.history.com/news/minimum-wage-america-timeline.

Mann, Heidi. "Seattle Small Businesswoman: I Know the $15 Minimum Wage is Bad for Business—It Has Devastated Mine." Fox News. February 7, 2019. Accessed June 7, 2021. www.foxnews.com/opinion/seattle-small-businesswoman-i-know-the-15-minimum-wage-is-bad-for-business-it-has-devastated-mine.

"Minimum Wage in America: How Many People are Earning $7.25 an Hour?" USAFacts. March 25, 2021. Accessed June 7, 2021. usafacts.org/articles/minimum-wage-america-how-many-people-are-earning-725-hour/.

Mourdoukoutas, Panos. "Seattle Reveals the Ugly Truth about the $15 Minimum Wage Movement." Forbes. June 28, 2017. Accessed June 7, 2021. www.forbes.com/sites/panosmourdoukoutas/2017/06/28/seattle-reveals-the-ugly-truth-about-the-15-minimum-wage-movement/?sh=39d9d0f062dc.

Phelan, John. "5 Reasons Raising the Minimum Wage Is Bad Public Policy" FEE Freeman Article. March 25, 2019. Accessed

June 7, 2021. fee.org/articles/5-reasons-raising-the-minimum
-wage-is-bad-public-policy/.

Chapter 16: Capitalism

Bandler, Aaron. "5 Statistics Showing How Capitalism Solves
Poverty." The Daily Wire. March 18, 2017. Accessed June 7,
2021. www.dailywire.com/news/5-statistics-showing-how
-capitalism-solves-poverty-aaron-bandler.

Carrasco, Jorge C. "How Free Market Capitalism Made Chile the
Richest Latin American Country." Free the People. October
25, 2018. Accessed June 7, 2021. freethepeople.org/how-free
-market-capitalism-made-chile-the-richest-latin-american
-country/.

Cost, Jay, and Allen Estrin. "What is Crony Capitalism?" PragerU.
February 22, 2016. Accessed June 7, 2021. www.prageru
.com/video/what-is-crony-capitalism/.

Horwitz, Steven. "Capitalism is Good for the Poor." FEE Freeman
Article. June 9, 2016. Accessed June 7, 2021. fee.org/articles
/capitalism-is-good-for-the-poor/.

Kurtz, Annalyn, and Tal Yellin. "These 10 Charts Show How the
Economy Performed under Trump versus Prior Presidents."
CNN. October 29, 2020. Accessed June 7, 2021. www.cnn
.com/interactive/2020/10/business/us-economy-trump-vs
-other-presidents/.

Nelson, Fraser. "What Oxfam Won't Tell You about Capitalism
and Poverty: 16 January 2017." The Spectator. January 16,
2017. Accessed June 7, 2021. blogs.spectator.co.uk/2017/01
/oxfam-wont-tell-capitalism-poverty/#.

"New Data Show Child Mortality Rates Falling Faster than Ever."
World Health Organization. September 16, 2014. Accessed
June 7, 2021. https://www.who.int/news/item/16-09-2014

-new-data-show-child-mortality-rates-falling-faster-than
-ever.

"Our History." Walmart. Accessed June 7, 2021. corporate.walmart
.com/our-story/our-history.

Tupy, Marian L. and Alexander Hammond. "5 Reasons Capitalist Chile is Better than Socialist Venezuela." FEE Freeman Article. May 20, 2019. Accessed June 7, 2021. fee.org
/articles/5-reasons-capitalist-chile-is-better-than-socialist
-venezuela/.

Chapter 17: A Vision for America

Brink, Susan. "What Country Spends the Most (And Least) On
Health Care per Person?" New Hampshire Public Radio.
Accessed June 7, 2021. www.nhpr.org/post/what-country
-spends-most-and-least-health-care-person#stream/0.

Gasulla, Sabrina. "Chicago's Wealth Divide." Crain's Chicago
Business. Accessed June 7, 2021. esrimedia.maps.arcgis.com
/apps/Cascade/index.html?appid=13f012b816fc417296410b
f957948703.

Ivanova, Irina. "Millennials Are the Biggest—but Poorest—
Generation." CBS News. November 26, 2019. Accessed June 7,
2021. www.cbsnews.com/news/millennials-have-just-3-of-us
-wealth-boomers-at-their-age-had-21/.

Kastrenakes, Jacob. "Amazon's Net Income Tripled Last Quarter, and It Didn't Even Have Prime Day to Help." The Verge.
October 29, 2020. Accessed June 7, 2021. www.theverge
.com/2020/10/29/21539921/amazon-q3-2020-earnings-net
-income-triple.

Sundaram, Anjali. "Yelp Data Shows 60% of Business Closures
Due to the Coronavirus Pandemic Are Now Permanent."
CNBC. December 11, 2020. Accessed June 7, 2021. www.cnbc

RESOURCES

.com/2020/09/16/yelp-data-shows-60percent-of-business
-closures-due-to-the-coronavirus-pandemic-are-now
-permanent.html.

"Vaccine Injury Compensation Data." Official Web Site of the
U.S. Health Resources & Services Administration. June 1, 2021.
Accessed June 7, 2021. www.hrsa.gov/vaccine-compensation
/data/index.html.

About the Author

· · · · · · · · · · · · · · · · ·

Will Witt is a media personality, national speaker, short film director, cultural commentator, and host of the show *Will Witt Live* on PragerU. A college dropout, Will Witt moved to Los Angeles to pursue a career in media and politics. In the span of a year and a half, Will Witt has amassed over five hundred million views of his online videos and is one of the most viewed conservative media personalities in America. Will Witt's first mini documentary, *Fleeing California*, has been viewed over seven million times. He has made frequent appearances on Fox News, the Daily Wire, and Blaze Media. He was featured on the cover of the *New York Times*, which discussed the massive impact he and PragerU have had on America. He lives in Los Angeles.